# CONTENTS

## Andalucía and the Costa del Sol Area by Area

## Streetsmart

Within each Top 10 list in this book, no hierarchy of quality or popularity is implied. All 10 are, in the editor's opinion, of roughly equal merit.

***Front cover and spine*** *The stunning Alhambra, Granada's medieval palace*
***Back cover*** *A stretch of the Cabo de Gata San Miguel shoreline, Almería*
***Title page*** *The beautiful village of Mijas on the Costa del Sol*

# Welcome to
# Andalucía and the Costa del Sol

Flamenco, wine, tapas, beaches, sunshine: everything that makes Spain one of the best-loved and most visited countries on Earth is concentrated in the region of Andalucía. But this beguiling region is also home to some of Europe's most romantic cities, its most important wetlands reserve and second-highest mountain range, offering a wealth of outdoor pursuits from hiking to skiing. With Eyewitness Top 10 Andalucía & the Costa del Sol, it's yours to explore.

Andalucía's three great cities – **Granada**, **Seville** and **Córdoba** – are important repositories of Spain's historical identity and symbols of the area's Moorish past, with world-class heritage sites such as the **Mezquita** in Córdoba, Granada's **Alhambra** and Seville's **Cathedral.** Other vibrant must-sees are **Jerez de la Frontera** and its sherry *bodegas* and **Ronda**, with its jaw-dropping location above the **Tajo** gorge, while **Baeza** and **Úbeda** are immaculately preserved towns full of Renaissance architecture. In between there are the famous *pueblos blancos*, or white villages, that dot the Andalucian hilltops.

Along the sun-drenched **Costa del Sol**, cultural and culinary riches are concentrated around **Málaga**, **Marbella** and **Gibraltar**. Between the dramatic "rock" and the ancient city of **Cádiz** lies the gorgeous **Costa de la Luz**, popular with Spanish tourists and windsurfers.

Whether you are here for a weekend or a week, our Top 10 guide provides everything you need to explore the region. Combine insider tips on what to do for free and where to stay with inspirational photography, detailed maps and easy-to-follow itineraries, and you have the ideal pocket companion. **Enjoy the book, and enjoy Andalucía and the Costa del Sol.**

Clockwise from top: The Alhambra, Granada; Sierra de Aracena; Alcázar, Seville; Cabo de Gata nature reserve; Andalucian wall tiles; Ronda atop the Tajo gorge; La Mezquita, Córdoba

# Exploring Andalucía and the Costa del Sol

The region offers a dizzying range of sights, sounds, flavours and fun. To start you off, here are ideas for a four- and seven-day tour.

## Four Days in Andalucía

### Day ❶

**MORNING**
Follow the dramatic winding A397 up through the coastal mountains of the Serranías Penibéticas to lunch in **Ronda** (see pp30–31). Take in the bullring, palaces and the view from the **Puente Nuevo** (see p30).

**AFTERNOON**
Drive to **Cádiz** (see pp26–7) and wander the backstreets of the medieval **Barrio del Pópulo**; don't miss the **Catedral Nueva** and the coastal promenade.

### Day ❷

**MORNING**
Explore the **Parque Nacional Doñana** (see pp36–7), catching the birdlife at dawn. Next visit **Jerez de la Frontera** (see p106) to sample the local sherries.

**AFTERNOON**
Enjoy the back-road route north via the *pueblo blanco* of **Arcos de la Frontera** (see p106) to **Seville** (see pp84–93) and its **Cathedral** and **La Giralda** (see pp18–19).

### Day ❸

**MORNING**
Visit Seville's **Real Alcázar** (see pp20–21) before driving on to the white village of **Carmona** (see p96), then on to **Córdoba** (see pp22–3).

**AFTERNOON**
Tour **La Mezquita** (see pp24–5), the **Jewish quarter** (see p22) and the **Alcázar de los Reyes Cristianos** (see p23).

**The Catedral Nueva** sits proudly above Cádiz seafront.

**Sierra de Cazorla** is a vast and diverse reserve.

**The impressive Alhambra** is a complex of Moorish fortresses and gardens.

**Key**
— Four-day itinerary
— Seven-day itinerary

**Arcos de la Frontera** is dramatically situated on a cliff edge.

## Day ④

Head to **Granada** (see pp116–123) to see the architectural complex and gardens of **the Alhambra** (see pp12–13) and **Generalife** (summer palace) (see pp14–15), then finally relax on the beach at **Nerja** (see p33).

## Seven Days in Andalucía

### Days ①–③ as above
### Day ④

Start at **the Alhambra** (see pp12–13), then explore the **Albaicín** quarter (see pp16–17), taking in the churches, Moorish baths and Moroccan tearooms. Afterwards, visit UNESCO-listed **Úbeda**'s Pottery Quarter (see p35), pretty plazas and Renaissance and Plateresque buildings.

### Day ⑤

Go for a short hike in the **Sierra de Cazorla** (see p61) and look out for birds of prey. Spend the evening in beautifully preserved **Baeza** (see p34), another UNESCO-listed site.

### Day ⑥

Discover the **Sierra Nevada** (see pp38–9), Europe's second-highest mountain range after the Alps. If it's summer, see the **Valle de Lecrín**'s olive, almond and citrus groves (see p39); in winter, you can go skiing.

### Day ⑦

Take the A41 south, along the western edge of the **Sierra Nevada** (see pp38–9) and enjoy the beach at **Nerja** (see p33) before visiting the market town of **Vélez-Málaga** (see pp33) on **the Costa del Sol**.

# Top 10 Andalucía and the Costa del Sol Highlights

The impressive Puente Nuevo
spans El Tajo gorge at Ronda

# 🔟 **Andalucía Highlights**

The diverse and politically semi-autonomous region of Andalucía has a population of 8.4 million and embodies what is thought of as typically Spanish. Memories of a visit here will be colourful, joyous and deeply stirring, and will likely include flamenco, remote white villages, sierras and sunny beaches.

0 kilometres 50

0 miles 50

Jabugo · Aracena · Cazalla de la Sierra ·

Minas de Riotinto · Lora del Río ·

**HUELVA**

Gibraleón · Seville · Alcalá de Guadaíra

Huelva ·

**SEVILLA**

Parque Nacional de Doñana ❾

Arcos de la Frontera ·

Jerez de la Frontera ·

**CÁDIZ**

Cádiz ❺ · San Fernando

Costa de la Luz

Algeciras

## **Moorish Granada**
Andalucía's 1,300-year-old Moorish heritage evokes pure Romanticism that is hard to equal. The delicate art and architecture are among the most splendid in Europe (see pp12–17).

## **Seville Cathedral and La Giralda**
These two chief wonders of Seville beautifully embody the juxtaposition of the Moors and their Christian conquerors (see pp18–19).

### **Real Alcázar, Seville** ❸
A mix of styles is evident in this luxurious palace, mostly built by Moorish artisans for Christians (see pp20–21).

## **Córdoba and La Mezquita**
This was once the most important Islamic city in Europe, a fact that is illustrated by the architectural masterpiece of La Mezquita, the Great Mosque (see pp22–5).

## **Cádiz** ❺
Said to be Europe's oldest city, Cádiz still retains an aura of age-old mystery. Its golden-domed cathedral is spectacular (see pp26–7).

### 6 Ronda

The largest of the *pueblos blancos* scattered throughout the region, Ronda is split by El Tajo gorge. It is also reputed to be the birthplace of the modern style of bullfighting *(see pp30–31)*.

### The Costa del Sol 7

From the wealthy yachting-set enclaves to package deals for families, this famous expanse of sand has something for everyone *(see pp32–3)*.

### Baeza and Úbeda 8

Both of these exquisite towns in Jaén Province offer world-class Renaissance architecture set in perfectly preserved historic centres *(see pp34–5)*.

### 9 Parque Nacional de Doñana

The vast delta of the Guadalquivir River is one of the world's most important nature reserves; without it birdlife throughout Europe would be seriously compromised *(see pp36–7)*.

### The Sierra Nevada 10

Europe's second-highest mountain range after the Alps offers its southernmost ski resort, a wealth of wildlife for trekkers, and dozens of remote traditional villages along its southern slopes *(see pp38–9)*.

# TOP 10 ⭐ Moorish Granada: the Alhambra

The great complex of the Alhambra is the best-preserved medieval Arab palace in the world and, with nearly two million visitors annually, it is also the most popular monument in Spain. Built on the largely inaccessible Sabika Hill overlooking the city of Granada, its most distinctive phase began in the 11th century as the *qa'lat al-Hamra* (Red Fort) of the Ziridian rulers. From the 13th to almost the end of the 15th century the kings of the succeeding Nasrid dynasty embellished the site in a most spectacular fashion.

The Alhambra, backed by the Sierra Nevada

### 1 Puerta de la Justicia
Built in 1348, the "Justice Gate" **(above)** horseshoe arch makes use of Arab defensive techniques – a steep approach combined with four right-angled turns – intended to slow down invading armies.

### 2 Puerta del Vino
The "Wine Gate" – so called because it was used as a wine cellar in the 16th century – marks what was once the main entrance arch to the Medina (market).

### 3 Plaza de los Aljibes
From these ramparts, visitors can enjoy superb views of Granada. The giant cisterns *(aljibes)* underneath were built by the Christian conquerors.

### 4 Alcazaba
Although largely in ruins, this fortress is well worth a look. Don't miss climbing up onto the Torre de la Vela for views of the Sierra Nevada.

### 5 Palacio de Carlos V
This Italian Renaissance palace **(left)** is the masterpiece of Pedro Machuca, a student of Michelangelo. Inside are the Museo de Bellas Artes and the Museo de la Alhambra, with its fine collection of Nasrid art.

### 6 Palacios Nazaríes

The Nasrid palaces are built of simple brick, wood and stucco, so as not to compete with the creations of Allah.

**Plan of the Alhambra**

Generalife

### 7 Palacio de Mexuar

The most poorly preserved of the three palaces, this was the most public space, dedicated to judicial and bureaucratic business. The original structure dates from 1365, but in the 16th century the Christians converted it to a chapel.

### 8 Palacio de Comares

Built in the mid-14th century, this area constituted the Serallo, where the sultan would receive dignitaries and deal with diplomatic issues. Inside is the Salón de Embajadores, the main throne room of the Alhambra. In front of the palace is the Patio de Arrayanes (right).

### 9 Palacio de los Leones

Dating from the late 1300s, this palace was the Harem, the private zone reserved for the sultan and his family. The fountain with 12 lions, in the central courtyard of the palace, may represent the 12 signs of the zodiac, the 12 hours of the clock, or the 12 tribes of Israel.

### 10 Partal

As you leave the Alhambra, stroll through the gardens with their watercourses laid out in an area that used to have palaces of its own. All you can see of them now are five porticoed arches (above). This area leads up to the Generalife (see pp14–15).

**NEED TO KNOW**

**MAP S2**

*The Alhambra:* 958 02 79 71. www.alhambra.org. Mid-Mar–mid-Oct: 8:30am–8pm daily, 10–11:30pm Tue–Sat; mid-Oct–mid-Mar: 8:30am–6pm daily, 8–9:30pm Fri–Sat; closed 1 Jan, 25 Dec. Adm: €14 (ticket window), €20 (online)

*Museo de la Alhambra*: 8:30am–6pm Wed–Sat (to 8pm mid-Mar–mid-Oct); 8:30am–2:30pm Tue & Sun; closed Mon, Jan 1, Dec 25. Night visits: May–Sep: 9–11:30pm Fri

■ Snacks and drinks are available, but taking water is a good idea.

■ Visitor numbers are restricted, so book tickets in advance online.

# Moorish Granada: Generalife

The Torre de los Picos

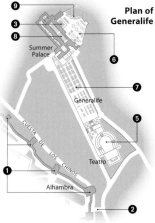

**Plan of Generalife**

## 1 The Towers

Following the gardens of the Partal *(see p13)* as you walk towards the Generalife, you will encounter a number of restored Moorish towers built into the wall. The Torre de los Picos, Torre del Cadí, Torre de la Cautiva, Torre de las Infantas, Torre del Cabo de la Carrera and Torre del Agua are all worth a look for their fine detail, as well as for the views they command. The Torre de la Cautiva and the Torre de las Infantas are twin tower-palaces with richly decorated rooms.

## 2 The Hill of the Sun

A footbridge flanked by two towers takes you over to the hill that rises above the Alhambra. A vast summer palace once stood here, amid 75 acres (30 ha) of gardens, which predated the Alhambra by more than a century, although little of it remains today.

## 3 Patio de los Cipreses

The Court of the Cypresses is also known as the Patio of the Sultana, for this is where Zoraya, the wife of Boabdil *(see p43)*, is said to have secretly met her lover, the chief of the Abencerrajes clan. The sultan had the chief's men massacred upon discovery of the infidelity. A 700-year-old cypress tree commemorates the trysting place.

## 4 The Name of the Garden

The word Generalife is generally considered to be a corruption of the Arab phrase *Djinat al-Arif*, which can be translated as "the Architect's Garden" (referring to Allah) or simply the "Best" or "High" garden. The Darro River was diverted 18 km (11 miles) to provide water for this lush sanctuary.

Patio de los Cipreses

## HISTORY OF THE ALHAMBRA

The castle was the last bastion of al-Andalus, the Moorish hegemony that, at its height, included almost the entire Iberian Peninsula. By 1237 the Christians had reconquered all but this emirate. The Moors managed to flourish for some 250 years longer, only falling to the forces of King Fernando and Queen Isabel in 1492 *(see p42)*. The Generalife was the summer palace where the Moorish leaders could escape political life and the bustling city below and relax in the landscaped grounds. After centuries of neglect, and attempts by Napoleon's army to blow up the palace, the structures were preserved in the early 19th century, after the American writer Washington Irving inspired the world with his *Tales of the Alhambra (see p49)*.

### 5 Teatro

As you climb the hill, you will encounter the amphitheatre, nestled into a tree-lined hollow. Dance performances and musical concerts are offered here as part of an annual festival of the arts.

### 6 Jardines Altos

As you reach the entrance to the upper gardens, you will encounter the Patio de Polo, where visitors would leave their horses before ascending to the palace.

**Wisteria in the Jardines Altos**

On this level there is a series of fountains and formal plantings, joined by walkways and copses.

### 7 Jardines Nuevos

It is clear the "New Gardens," also called the Lower Gardens, owe little to Moorish taste. Hedges and formal patterns echo Italian style, but the sound of running water creates an atmosphere in keeping with the Moorish ideal. In Islam, Paradise is defined as an oasis – a water garden full of blossoms.

**Patio de la Acequia fountains**

### 8 Patio de la Acequia

The "Court of the Long Pool" is the most famous water spectacle of the garden. Perfectly proportioned pools are set off by rows of water jets. At one end stands one of the complex's most harmonious buildings, the Sala Regia, with its decorated arcades and airy portico.

### 9 Escalera del Agua

These staircases above the palace, also known as the Camino de las Cascadas, have handrails that double as watercourses. It is best viewed in spring.

### 10 Leaving the Gardens

As you exit the gardens you will pass along the Paseo de las Adelfas and the Paseo de los Cipreses, lined respectively with oleanders and cypresses. Back to the Hill of the Sun, stroll down the pretty Cuesta del Rey Chico to the Albaicín *(see pp16–17)*.

# Moorish Granada: Albaicín

**Mudéjar-style Iglesia de Santa Ana**

## 1 Iglesia de Santa Ana
MAP R2 ■ C/Santa Ana 1

At the end of Plaza Nueva stands this 16th-century brick church in Mudéjar style, built by Muslim artisans for Christian patrons. Inside the main chapel is a coffered ceiling in the Moorish tradition. The bell tower was originally a minaret.

## 2 Paseo de los Tristes
MAP S2

The broad tree-lined esplanade follows the course of the river upstream. It once accommodated tournaments, processions and funeral cortèges, but now bars and restaurants dominate the scene.

## 3 Casa de Castril
MAP R2 ■ Carrera del Darro 43 ■ Centro Cultural CajaGranada: Av de la Ciencia 2 ■ 600 14 31 41 ■ Closed for renovation

This ornate 16th-century mansion was originally owned by the secretary to King Fernando and Queen Isabel. Since 1879 it has served as the Archaeological and Ethnological Museum, displaying artifacts from Granada's past, from the Paleolithic era up until the Reconquest in 1492. Although it is currently closed for renovations, some of its finest pieces are on show at the Centro Cultural CajaGranada.

## 4 Iglesia de San Pedro y San Pablo
MAP R2 ■ Carrera del Darro 2

Across from the Casa de Castril, this church, built in the 1500s, graces an attractive spot on the banks of the river. From here you can see the Alhambra dominating the landscape.

## 5 Real Chancillería
MAP Q2 ■ Plaza del Padre Suárez 1

The austerely impressive Royal Chancery dates from 1530, built shortly after the *reconquista* as part of the futile attempt to Christianize this Moorish quarter. The palace is attributed to architect Diego de Siloé.

**Real Chancillería, now the high court**

## 6 El Bañuelo (Baños Árabes)
MAP R2 ■ Carrera del Darro 31 ■ 958 22 97 38 ■ Open 10am–2pm Tue–Sat

Dating from the 11th century, these are the best preserved Moorish baths in Spain. They comprise several rooms that were used for changing, meeting, massage and bathing.

**The old Moorish baths of El Bañuelo**

**El Mirador de San Nicolás, offering fine views of the Alhambra**

### 7 El Mirador de San Nicolás
MAP R1

In front of the Iglesia de San Nicolás, this magnificent terrace has such lovely views of the Alhambra and the Sierra Nevada that it has long been dubbed El Mirador ("The Lookout Point") de San Nicolás. The views are extraordinary at sunset, when the Alhambra glows softly ochre and the often snowcapped Sierra Nevada radiates pink in the distance.

### 8 Plaza Larga
MAP R1

From the Paseo de los Tristes follow Calle Panaderos to reach this busy market square, where you'll find mostly produce stalls as well as cheap eateries and bars. The square sports an Islamic gateway with a typically angled entrance as part of what remains of the upper fortifications. This is the Arco de las Pesas – if you pass through it you will come to the Albaicín's most popular square, Plaza San Nicolás.

**Map of Albaicín**

### 9 Tearooms

As you wander around the labyrinth of whitewashed houses and tiny sloping alleyways of the Albaicín quarter you will encounter many tearooms – a Moroccan tradition that is very much alive in this quarter. Possibly the best one, La Tetería del Bañuelo (see p122), consists of a series of rooms set amid delightful gardens. Here you can sip your minty brew, nibble honeyed sweets and contemplate the timeless panorama.

### 10 Moroccan Shops

Check out the hilly streets off Calle Elvira, especially Caldería Vieja and Caldería Nueva, for typically Moroccan shops. The scene is indistinguishable from what you would find in Morocco itself, with the colourful wares spilling out onto the pavements (see p120).

---

**SACROMONTE GYPSY CAVES**

Leaving the Albaicín quarter to the north, follow the Camino del Sacromonte to reach the hill of the same name. The so-called "Holy Hill" is most noted for the presence of some 3,500 caves traditionally inhabited by gypsies (see p46). For more than six centuries, the zone has been notorious for wild goings-on, most especially *zambras*, impromptu gypsy fiestas of flamenco music and dance, and outsiders have always been welcome to witness their cultural celebrations. Today some 80 per cent of the caves are still occupied and several of them continue to operate as venues for tourist spectacles.

# TOP 10 ★ Seville Cathedral and La Giralda

In 1248, after some 500 years of Islamic rule, Seville was reconquered by Christian forces, who threatened the Moorish inhabitants with full-scale massacre if they damaged any of the city's magnificent edifices. Pragmatically, the conquerors simply rededicated the huge Almohad mosque to the Virgin and for about 150 years used it as their principal place of worship. In 1401, the building was demolished. It took just over a century to erect a new cathedral of unprecedented proportions on its rectangular base.

### 1 Exterior and Scale

In sheer cubic vastness, Seville Cathedral **(right)** is the largest Christian church in the world, and there's a certificate from the Guinness Book of Records on display here to prove it. It measures 126 m (415 ft) by 83 m (270 ft) and the nave rises to 43 m (140 ft). The best place to take it all in is from La Giralda.

### 2 Cathedral Paintings

There are around 600 paintings throughout the cathedral, from the entrance pavilion to the sacristies, together with sculptures from the 17th-century Sevillian School, which included artists Bartolomé Esteban Murillo, Francisco de Zurbarán and Francisco Pacheco.

### 3 Puerta del Perdón

The "Gate of Forgiveness" is set in a crenellated wall and is the main entrance to the one surviving part of the mosque. The arch and bronze doors are a masterpiece of Almohad art, carved with 880 Koranic inscriptions. Sculpted Renaissance elements include a bas-relief of the Expulsion of the Moneychangers from the Temple.

### 4 Sacristía de los Cálices

Part of the cathedral's treasury is housed here. The anteroom displays the Tenebrario, a 7.8-m (25-ft) Plateresque candelabrum used during Holy Week. Inside, the star turns are a painting by Goya of Seville's patron saints, Justa and Rufina, as well as canvases by Zurbarán, Jordaens and other Masters.

### 5 Sacristía Mayor

The Main Sacristy **(left)** is dominated by a dome, designed in the 16th century. The centrepiece of the sacristy is a 450-kg (990-lb), 3-m (10-ft) silver Baroque monstrance created by Juan de Arfe.

**6** **Patio de los Naranjos**
The Courtyard of Orange Trees was the place where ritual ablutions were performed before entering the mosque for prayer.

**7** **Interior**
The vast Gothic arches that line the nave inside the cathedral are so high that the space within the building is said to have its own independent climate.

**8** **La Giralda**
This grand tower **(below)** is the symbol of Seville, built between 1172 and 1195. It takes its name from the weathervane on top, called *El Giraldillo*.

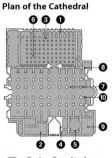

### SEMANA SANTA FESTIVITIES

Seville's Holy Week celebrations leading up to Easter *(see p80)* are Andalucía's richest. Here, 61 *cofradías* (brotherhoods) compete to bear aloft the most well-dressed Virgin in mourning and an image from the Passion of Christ. Floats are carried by *costaleros* (bearers), while the processions are lead by *nazarenos* – penitents in hoods.

**Plan of the Cathedral**

**9** **Sala Capitular**
The Chapter House contains Murillo's *Immaculate Conception* in the vault and boasts a lavish marble floor.

**10** **Capilla Mayor**
The main altar's *tour de force* is its 15th-century *retablo* – the world's largest altarpiece **(below)**. Composed of gilded carved wood, it features some 45 Biblical scenes employing some 1,000 figures.

**NEED TO KNOW**

**MAP M4** ■ Plaza Virgen de los Reyes ■ 954 21 49 71 ■ www.catedralde sevilla.es; guided tours and rooftop tours: www. cubiertasdelacatedral.com; audioguides free 4:30–6pm Mon with reservation

**Open** 11am–3:30pm Mon, 11am–5pm Tue–Sat, 2:30–6pm Sun; services:

Oct–May: 8:30am Mon–Fri (Capilla Real), 9am Mon–Fri (Capilla de la Antigua)

Adm: €9 (includes access to La Giralda)

■ For great views head to the rooftop bar at EME Catedral Hotel *(see p140)*.

■ It's an easy-going climb up La Giralda, on ramps.

# 🔟⭐ Real Alcázar, Seville

This extensive complex embodies a series of palatial rooms and spaces from various ages. The front towers and walls are the oldest surviving section, dating from AD 913 and built by the Emir of Córdoba, Abd ar-Rahman III, most likely on the ruins of Roman barracks. A succession of caliphs added their dazzling architectural statements over the ensuing centuries. Then came the Christian kings, particularly Pedro I in the 14th century, and finally the rather perfunctory 16th-century apartments of Carlos V.

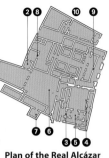

**Plan of the Real Alcázar**

### 1 Puerta del León

The entrance gate into the first courtyard **(above)** is flanked by original Almohad walls. Note the Gothic and Arabic inscriptions on the interior façade.

### 2 Sala de Justicia

Here and in adjacent halls and courts is some of the purest Mudéjar art commissioned by Alfonso XI of Castile around 1330 and executed by craftsmen from Granada. The star-shaped coffered ceiling and fine plasterwork are quite exquisite.

### 3 Patio de las Muñecas

The intimate Courtyard of the Dolls was the private living room of the palace and supposedly gets its name from two faces carved into the base of one of the arches.

### 4 Patio de las Doncellas

The Courtyard of the Maidens **(above)** commemorates the annual tribute of 100 virgins delivered to the Moorish rulers by the Christians. Look out for the fine *azulejos* (tiles).

### 5 Salón de Embajadores

The most brilliant room in the entire Alcázar. Its crowning glory is the dazzling dome of carved, painted and gilded wood **(above)**, constructed by craftsmen from Toledo and completed in 1366.

### 6 Patio de la Montería

The Hunting Courtyard has 14th-century Mudéjar decorative work – a perfect mix of cultural influences.

### 7 Casa de la Contratación

The halls in the House of Trade are where Fernando and Isabel met with the explorers of the New World.

### 8 Patio del Yeso

The secluded Courtyard of Plaster, greatly restored, is one of the few remnants of the 12th-century palace. The delicate stucco work features scalloped arches **(right)** and is set off by a garden with water channels.

### 9 Palacio Gótico

In a refurbished 13th-century Gothic structure built by Alfonso X the Wise, this palace has a rather inharmonious Renaissance style.

### 10 Gardens

Moorish touches – fountains, pools, orange groves, palms and hedgerows – abound in these gardens **(left)**. Concerts and events are held here on summer evenings.

---

**NEED TO KNOW**

**MAP M4** ■ Patio de Banderas ■ 954 50 23 24 ■ www.alcazarsevilla.org

**Open** Apr–Sep: 9:30am–7pm daily; Oct–Mar: 9:30am–5pm daily; closed 1 & 6 Jan,

Good Friday, 25 Dec

Adm: €9.50; free Mon (Apr–Sep: 6–7pm; Oct–Mar: 4–5pm)

■ A flow-control entry system allows a limited number of people into the Alcázar every half hour.

■ To avoid long waits, visit at off-peak times.

■ There are dramatized 30-minute evening tours with re-enactments of important moments in the Alcázar's history; book tickets in advance.

# TOP10 ⭐ Córdoba

The main sight in Córdoba is undoubtedly the Great Mosque, La Mezquita – one of the unsurpassed masterpieces of world architecture. But the entire city is a jewel in Andalucía's crown. In addition to the mosque and its incongruous but splendid cathedral within, other sights here include fine monuments and palaces from every age, art and history museums, one of Andalucía's greatest archaeological repositories, and a museum dedicated to the history of the bullfight.

### ③ Judería

All around the Mezquita is the city's ancient Jewish quarter **(left)**, dating back to the time of the Roman Empire. Its narrow alleyways are brilliantly whitewashed, hung with flowerpots, and graced with beautiful Moorish patios. This district also has Andalucía's only medieval synagogue.

### ④ Palacio de los Marqueses de Viana

A former noble residence (14th- to 18th-century), the museum includes preserved period rooms and furnishings.

### ① La Mezquita

The world's third-largest mosque remains a place of immense grandeur and mystical power *(see pp24–5)*.

### ② Plaza del Potro

This small but elegant square, adorned with a 16th-century fountain, was once Córdoba's livestock market.

### ⑤ Baños del Alcázar Califal

Built in the 10th century, these Arab baths **(right)** use the classical order of Roman baths, with cold, warm and hot rooms.

---

**NEED TO KNOW**

**MAP D3**

*Alcázar and Baños:* Campo Santo de los Mártires. 957 42 01 51. Summer: 8:30am–2:30pm Tue–Sat, 9:30am–2:30pm Sun & hols; winter: 8:30am– 8:45pm Tue–Fri, 8:30am– 4:30pm Sat (to 2:30pm Sun). Adm: Alcázar €4.50 (€7 Mon); Baños €2.50

*Museo de Bellas Artes:* Plaza del Potro 1. 957 10 36 59. Summer: 9am–3:30pm Tue–Sun; winter: 9am–8:30pm Tue–Sat (to 3:30pm Sun). Adm: €1.50

*Museo Arqueológico:* Plaza Jerónimo Páez 7. 957 35 55 17. Open as Museo de Bellas Artes. Adm: €1.50

*Palacio de los Marqueses de Viana:* Plaza Don Gome 2. 957 49 67 41. Summer: 9am–3pm Tue–Sun; winter: 10am–7pm Tue–Sat (to 3pm Sun). Adm: €8

*Museo Torre de la Calahorra:* Puente Romano. 957 29 39 29. May–Sep: 10am–2pm, 4:30–8:30pm daily; Oct–Apr: 10am–6pm daily. Adm: €4.50

**Map of Córdoba**

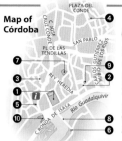

### 7 Museo Arqueológico

Housed in a Renaissance mansion is this excellent archaeological museum. One highlight is the 10th-century Moorish bronze of a stag, which was found at Medina Azahara (see p125).

(see p125)

---

**MULTICULTURAL TRADITION**

Córdoba's brilliance owes much to its rich multicultural history. Its most important edifices are emblematic of the cross-fertilization of Islamic, Christian and Jewish cultures. In the 10th century, Córdoba was the spiritual and scientific centre of the Western World, due to its policy of religious tolerance (see p42). After the reconquista, many non-Christian thinkers were banished and the city fell into decline.

(see p42)

### 8 Puente Romano

Crossing the Río Guadalquivir, this bridge (left) has Roman foundations. Halfway across, a statue honours Archangel Raphael, said to have saved the city from the plague.

### 6 Museo Torre de la Calahorra

Part of a Moorish castle that controlled access to the city, the tower now houses the Roger Garaudy Three Cultures Museum, which explains how all religions lived side by side in medieval Córdoba and houses exhibits from the time (right). There are great views of the city from the tower.

### 9 Museo de Bellas Artes

A former 16th-century charity hospital is now the city's main art museum. It has a collection of works by local painters and sculptors, as well as paintings and drawings by masters such as Goya, Ribera, Murillo, Valdés Leal and Zurbarán.

### 10 Alcázar de los Reyes Cristianos

This fortified palace, built in 1328, was used by the Inquisition (1500s–1820) and as a prison (until the 1950s). But today it is tranquil, with gardens, water terraces and fountains (left).

# 🔟 ⭐ La Mezquita, Córdoba

Although it has officially been a Christian site for almost nine centuries, La Mezquita's identity as a mosque is inescapable – notwithstanding the cathedral insensitively placed in its centre like a huge spider in its web. As with the Alhambra (see pp12–13), Emperor Carlos V can be blamed for this aesthetic transgression. Overriding the wishes of Córdoba's mayor, Carlos authorized the cathedral's construction in the 16th century, although he deeply regretted his decision when he saw the completed travesty.

## 1 The Caliphal Style

The mosque was begun by Caliph Abd el-Rahman I in AD 786. La Mezquita constitutes the beginning of the Caliphal architectural style, combining Roman, Gothic, Byzantine, Syrian and Persian elements.

## 2 Puerta del Perdón

Originally the mosque had many entrances, designed to let in light. The Gate of Forgiveness (1377) is now the only one open to all **(above)**.

## 3 Torre del Alminar

A minaret once stood where the belfry now is **(right)**. Built in 957, it was enveloped in this Baroque bell tower.

## 4 Interior

The plan of the interior **(above)** is that of a so-called "forest" mosque, with the rows and rows of variegated columns (856 remaining) and arches designed to resemble palm trees. Unlike Christian churches, based on earlier Roman basilicas with their focus on the central enthroned "judge", the Islamic aim is to induce a meditative state for prayer.

## ⑤ Patio de los Naranjos

The delightful Courtyard of the Orange Trees would have been used by worshippers to perform ritual ablutions before they went to prayer.

## ⑥ Recycled Columns

Great ingenuity was required to achieve the rhythmic uniformity inside, since most of the columns used in construction were recycled from Roman, Visigothic and other sources. They were a hotchpotch of varying sizes, so the longer ones had to be sunk into the floor. To reach the desired height, a second tier was then added.

## ⑦ Capilla de Villaviciosa and Capilla Real

One of the happier Christian additions, the Villaviciosa Chapel **(above)**, built in 1377, has exuberant Mudéjar arches. Next to it, the Royal Chapel has stucco work and *azulejos* (tiles).

**A SPIRITUAL SITE**

This magnificent edifice was not the first religious structure to be built on this spot. The Caliph bought the land from the Christians, who had built the Visigothic Cathedral of St Vincent here. In its last years, that building had been divided by a partition, so that it could serve the needs of both Christian and Muslim communities. The Visigothic structure, in its turn, had been constructed on top of a Roman temple, and its columns are still visible in La Mezquita.

## ⑧ Mihrab

Dating from the 10th century, this is the jewel of the mosque. An octagonal chamber set into the wall, it was to be the sacred focal point of prayer, directed towards Mecca. No amount of ornamentation was spared. Emperor Nicephorus III sent artisans from Constantinople to create some of the finest Byzantine mosaics in existence **(right)**.

**NEED TO KNOW**

**MAP D3** ■ Calle del Cardenal Herrero 1, Córdoba ■ 957 47 05 12 ■ www.mezquita decordoba.org

**Open** Mar–Oct: 10am–7pm Mon–Sat, 8:30–11:30am & 3–7pm Sun & hols; Nov–Feb: 8:30am–6pm Mon–Sat, 8:30–11:30am & 3–6pm Sun & hols

Adm: adults €8; children aged 10–14 €4; under 10s free

■ Last admission is 30 minutes before closing, but try to allow at least an hour to do the site justice.

■ El Caballo Rojo (C/Cardenal Herrero 28 • 957 47 53 75 • €€€) is located just across from the Puerta del Perdón. The restaurant is a local favourite, and many recipes are Moorish influenced. Dine on the terrace for views of the mosque.

## ⑨ Cathedral

In 1523, some 60 of the 1,013 columns were removed from the mosque to make way for the cathedral.

## ⑩ Choir Stalls

The Baroque choir stalls date from 1758, and the exquisite carved mahogany depicts Biblical scenes.

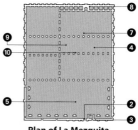

**Plan of La Mezquita**

# Cádiz

Cádiz inspired the poet Lord Byron to praise its heavenly blue setting, gorgeous women and sensuous lifestyle. Nowadays it is one of Andalucía's under-visited treasures. According to ancient chronicles, the city was founded by the Phoenicians as Gadir ("Fortress") in 1104 BC, giving it a good claim to being Europe's oldest. Under the Romans it became Gades and was notable as the city where Julius Caesar held his first public office.

**Map of Cádiz**

### 3 Barrio del Pópulo

The Barrio del Pópulo is the medieval heart of the city, which still retains its three 13th-century gates. The main entrance of the surviving 18th-century city wall, the Puerta de Tierra **(left)**, marks the boundary between the old city and the modern part of Cádiz.

### 5 Torre Tavira

The camera obscura in this tower, the city's highest at 46 m (150 ft), offers great views.

### 6 Oratorio de la Santa Cueva

This elliptical Neo-Classical chapel has an upper church with Ionic columns. Three frescoes by Goya depict miraculous moments from the life of Christ.

### 1 Iglesia de Santa Cruz and Teatro Romano

In the midst of the Barrio del Pópulo are ruins of a Roman theatre and a church dating from 1260.

### 2 Hospital de Mujeres

This Baroque former hospital's main attraction is El Greco's *Extasis de San Francisco*.

### 4 Plaza de las Flores

Also known as the Plaza de Topete, this square **(right)** was the sight of a Phoenician temple.

**LOS CARNAVALES**

The vibrant Carnaval celebrations in this port town are the most exhilarating in all of Spain *(see p80)*. In fact, so dear is this annual blow-out to *gaditanos* (as the locals call themselves) that it was the only such event in the country that Franco's forces failed to suppress during the decades of dictatorship. The festival's various traditions date back to the 15th century, when the town had a Genoese enclave, though some claim there is also a strong Cuban influence.

 **Catedral Nueva**
The "New Cathedral" **(above)** was begun in 1722. The bell tower, or Torre de Poniente (western tower), offers superb views of the city below.

**NEED TO KNOW**

**MAP B5**

*Catedral Nueva*: 956 28 61 54. 10am–7pm Mon–Sat, 1:30–7pm Sun. Adm: €5

*Torre de Poniente*: 10am–6pm daily (to 8pm mid-Jun–mid-Sep). Adm: €5

*Torre Tavira*: C/Marqués del Real Tesoro 10. 956 21 29 10. 10am–6pm daily (to 8pm May–Sep). Adm: €6

*Hospital de Mujeres*: Calle Hospital de Mujeres 26. 956 22 36 47. Summer: 8am–1:30pm Mon–Fri; winter: 10am–1:30pm & 5:30–8pm Mon–Fri

*Museo de Cádiz*: Plaza Mina. 856 10 50 23. Mid-Jun–mid-Sep: 9am–3:30pm Tue–Sun & hols; mid-Sep–mid-Jun: 9am–8:30pm Tue–Sat (to 3:30pm Sun & hols). Adm: €1.50 (free for EU members)

■ Book hotels up to a year ahead for Carnaval.

**⑧ Museo de Cádiz**
Archaeological finds and Baroque paintings are the museum's forte. Exhibits include Roman shipwreck finds and a pair of 5th-century BC Phoenician sarcophagi, showing Greek and Egyptian influences.

**⑩ Museo de las Cortes de Cádiz**
A mural in this museum eulogizes Cádiz as the birthplace of liberalism. On 29 March 1812, Spain's first liberal constitution was drawn up here; it played a huge role in shaping modern European politics.

**⑨ Plaza San Juan de Dios**
On the edge of the Barrio del Pópulo is this palm-fringed plaza **(below)**, dating from the 16th century. Facing the port, it forms the hub of city life.

# TOP 10 ⭐ Ronda

This is the most famous of the *pueblos blancos* – a scattering of evocative hamlets that reveal their Moorish roots between Málaga, Algeciras and Seville *(see p102)*. Ronda is the only town in the wildly mountainous region of the Serranía de Ronda. Located just half an hour's drive from the Costa del Sol, Ronda hosts up to 75,000 tourists per day, yet has managed to retain its timelessness and charm. Its natural setting is so spectacular that the views alone make it a must-see experience.

### 1 El Tajo and Puente Nuevo

Ronda perches upon a sheer outcrop that is split by a precipitous cleft, El Tajo, 100 m (330 ft) deep **(right)**. The spectacular 18th-century Puente Nuevo bridge links the old city, La Ciudad, with the new.

### 2 Casa del Rey Moro

A visit to the gardens of this 18th-century mansion, built on the foundations of a Moorish palace, will provide wonderful views.

### 3 Baños Árabes

These wonderfully preserved Moorish baths **(above)** date from the 1200s or early 1300s. The multiple barrel vaulting pierced with star-shaped lunettes is typical of such structures, but the octagonal brick columns supporting horseshoe arches are highly original.

### 4 Palacio del Marqués de Salvatierra

The carved stone portal outside this private 18th-century mansion features four squat figures that may represent South American Indians.

**NEED TO KNOW**
**MAP D5**

*Casa del Rey Moro*: C/ Santo Domingo 9. 952 16 10 02. www.turismoderonda.es. Gardens only: 10am–8pm daily. Adm: €5

*Baños Árabes*: Barrio de Padre Jesús. 656 95 09 37. 10am–7pm Mon–Fri (to 6pm Oct–Mar), 10am–3pm Sat, Sun & hols. Adm: €3

*Museo del Bandolero*: C/ Armiñán 65. 952 87 77 85.

11am–8:30pm daily (to 7pm winter). Adm: €3.75

*Iglesia de Santa María la Mayor*: Plaza Duquesa de Parcent. 952 87 22 46. 10am–7pm Mon–Sat, 10am–12:30pm & 2–7pm hols. Adm: €4

*Palacio de Mondragón*: 952 87 08 18. 10am–6pm Mon–Fri. Adm: €3

*Plaza de Toros*: C/Virgen de la Paz 15. 952 87 41 32. www.rmcr.org. Adm: €7

*Previous pages* The Alhambra with a backdrop of the Sierra Nevada

### 5 Palacio de Mondragón

One of Ronda's most beautiful palaces dates from 1314. Some of the original mosaic work, a magnificent Mudéjar ceiling and shady inner courtyards **(left)** can still be seen. Part of the palace is now the city's archaeological museum.

**THE ORIGINS OF BULLFIGHTING**

The creation here of the Real Maestranza de Caballería (Royal Academy of Knights) in 1572 set the stage for the birth of bullfighting. The Maestranza trained Spain's aristocracy to ride and students on horseback would challenge wild bulls. Legend tells that when one rider fell from his horse and was attacked by a bull, a bystander distracted the animal by waving his hat. The man's grandson, Pedro Romero (1749–1839), perfected the art.

**Map of Ronda**

### 6 Puente Viejo and Puente de San Miguel

The Puente Viejo (Old Bridge) dates from 1616 and may be a rebuilding of a Roman span across the gorge, though some say that its pedigree is Moorish, like the Puente de San Miguel.

### 7 Minarete de San Sebastián

This graceful 14th-century tower is all that remains of a Nasrid mosque and the church of San Sebastián that was built on top of it.

### 8 Plaza de Toros

Inaugurated in 1785, Ronda's bullring **(left)** was constructed in limestone in an elegant double-tiered sweep; it is the widest in the world and one of the oldest in Spain. Ronda is the birthplace and spiritual home of Spanish bullfighting, and houses a museum – the Museo Taurino – dedicated to the tradition.

### 9 Museo del Bandolero

For 1,000 years, the Sierras were the haunt of bands of rebels and outlaws. The museum chronicles the history of notorious brigands.

### 10 Iglesia de Santa María la Mayor

Much of this church incorporates a 13th-century mosque, notably the base of the Mudéjar belfry.

# ⭐ The Costa del Sol

The former fishing villages of the "Sun Coast" welcome millions of international visitors each year – not counting the estimated 300,000 expats who call the coast home. The winning formula is 320 sunny days a year, warm waters and beaches, and good-value, though somewhat brash, entertainment options. Heavy on neon and tower blocks, most of what's here has little to do with local culture, but what is exuberantly Andalucian is the verve with which visitors enjoy themselves in the sun – and party well into the night.

**① Estepona**
The first major resort on this coast is an excellent quieter choice, with 19 km (12 miles) of beach. In the *casco antiguo* (old town), Plaza Las Flores retains considerable charm.

**② Marbella**
The 15th-century Plaza de los Naranjos is the heart of old town Marbella, Spain's most expensive resort. Nearby Puerto Banús is the town's glittering marina **(right)**, where you can admire the fabulous yachts and mingle with the super-rich.

**⑤ Mijas**
Visit this beautiful little village nestled in the mountains **(left)** for views of the coast, as well as the maze of old Moorish streets filled with charming shops in its tiny squares.

**③ Fuengirola**
This large resort is the most family-orientated, with a good beach and a seafront promenade. There is a restored 10th-century Moorish castle.

**④ Benalmádena**
This resort comes in three parts: the old town inland; the beach and port area **(right)**; and Arroyo de la Miel, a lively suburb.

## 6 Torremolinos

Torre de los Molinos (Tower of the Windmills) refers to a Moorish watchtower that was once surrounded by 19 flourmills. The ancient Torre Vigia is still here, but surrounding it now is a big, brash and trashily modern resort that is the quintessence of inexpensive fun.

## 7 Málaga

Andalucía's second largest city (above) has invested €100m in the arts in the last ten years and boasts outposts of Paris's Pompidou Centre and the State Russian Museum – part of a "mile of art". The redeveloped waterfront has given Málaga dozens of new dining options.

## 8 Torre del Mar

Favoured by Spanish families, this resort is less tawdry than others to the west. It has a wide sandy beach backed by a tree-lined promenade.

### FRANCO'S DREAM

It was General Franco, Spain's dictator until 1975, who had the idea of transforming the impoverished fishing villages into the "Florida of Europe". He enacted his plan in the 1960s with money loaned by the US, in return for the right to build nuclear bases on Spanish soil. The jet-set glamour and cheap package deals were a runaway success and by the 1970s the area was an aesthetic and environmental disaster. Since the 1980s, steps have been taken to clean it up.

## 9 Vélez-Málaga

This market town has beautiful Mudéjar features and a lively annual flamenco guitar competition every July.

## 10 Nerja

Tasteful, white-washed Nerja (above) sits on attractive, verdant cliffs with quiet pebble beach coves below.

**Map of the Costa del Sol**

**NEED TO KNOW**

**MAP D5–E5**

*Estepona:* Tourist office, Avda de las Flores. 952 80 20 02

*Marbella:* Tourist office, Glorieta de la Fontanilla. 952 77 14 42

*Mijas:* Tourist office, Plaza Virgen de la Peña 2. 952 58 90 34

*Fuengirola:* Tourist office, Paseo Jesús Santos Rein 6. 952 46 74 57

*Benalmádena:* Tourist office, Avda Antonio Machado 10. 952 44 24 94

*Torremolinos:* Tourist office, Plaza Blas Infante 1. 952 37 95 12

*Málaga:* Tourist office, Pasaje de Chinitas 4. 951 30 89 11

*Nerja:* Tourist office, Calle Carmen 1. 952 52 15 31

# TOP 10 ⭐ Baeza and Úbeda

These two Jaén Province towns, only 9 km (5.5 miles) apart, are like matching jewel boxes overflowing with Renaissance architectural treasure, and so were awarded the title of UNESCO World Heritage Sites in 2003. Of the two, quiet Baeza has managed to stay almost completely out of the modern age, while Úbeda is now a thriving town with many seasonal attractions. Nevertheless, its stunning historic district is, if anything, the more spectacular.

### Plaza del Pópulo, Baeza ①
The town's most charming area, the Plaza del Pópulo, is in the midst of Renaissance edifices. It is also called the Square of the Lions, after its fountain, which has four stone lions and a female figure **(right)**.

### ② Puerta de Jaén, Baeza
A section of the ancient wall, the Jaén Gate, supports an additional arch with coats-of-arms set above.

### ③ Plaza Santa María and Catedral, Baeza
Several glorious 16th-century structures, including the cathedral, front this square. One of the many masterpieces by Renaissance architect Andrés de Vandelvira, the cathedral was originally a Gothic church, built over a mosque in the 13th century.

### ④ Paseo de la Constitución, Baeza
The 16th-century Alhóndiga (Corn Exchange) has elegant three-tiered arches, while the Torre de los Aliatares is an ancient remnant of the old wall.

### ⑤ Palacio de Jabalquinto, Baeza
One of the most unusually decorated palaces, the 15th-century Palacio de Jabalquinto **(left)** is sprinkled with coats of arms and stone studs in Isabelline Plateresque style.

### 6 Plaza San Lorenzo, Úbeda
The Casa de las Torres features two vast square towers with gargoyles, while the Church of San Lorenzo rests on the parapet of the old wall.

### 7 Plaza de San Pedro, Úbeda
Visit the patio of the Real Monasterio de Santa Clara, the town's oldest church **(right)**, where the nuns will sell you their distinctly Arabic *dulces* (sweetcakes). The Palacio de la Rambla is another Vandelvira creation, now home to a luxury hotel *(see pp144)*.

### 8 The Pottery Quarter, Úbeda
Passing through the Puerta del Losal, a splendid 13th-century Mudéjar gate, takes you into the town's age-old pottery quarter. Here, modern ceramic artists renowned all over Spain and beyond ply their ancient trade **(above)**.

### 9 Plaza del Primero de Mayo, Úbeda
The variety of riches here includes the Iglesia de San Pablo, displaying an array of styles, the 15th-century Casa Mudéjar – now an archaeological museum – and the 16th-century Ayuntamiento Viejo, with its superb arcades.

> **ARCHITECTURE OF THE SPANISH RENAISSANCE**
>
> Spanish Renaissance architecture divides into three periods: Plateresque, Classical High Renaissance and Herrerean. The first refers to the carved detailing on silverwork (*platero* means silversmith), a carry-over from the late Gothic style popular under Queen Isabel (Isabelline Plateresque). The High Renaissance style is noted for its symmetry and its Greco-Roman imagery. Herrerean works are very sober, practically devoid of decoration.

### 10 Plaza de Vázquez de Molina, Úbeda
Notable on this square is the Capilla del Salvador **(below)**. The Plateresque main front, by Vandelvira, marks a high point in the Spanish Renaissance.

**NEED TO KNOW**
**MAP F2**

***Baeza***: Tourist office, Casa del Pópulo, Plaza del Pópulo. 953 77 99 82. www.todosobrebaeza.com. 9am–7:30pm Mon–Fri, 9:30am–3pm Sat, Sun & hols

***Úbeda***: Tourist office, Palacio del Marqués de Contadero, C/Baja del Marqués 4. 953 77 92 04. www.ubedainteresa.com. 9am–7:30pm Mon–Fri, 9:30am–3pm Sat, Sun & hols

■ In Úbeda, have a drink in the courtyard of the Parador Condestable Dávalos *(see p142)*.

■ Baeza's Restaurante Juanito (*Avda del Alcalde Puché Pardo 57 • 953 74 00 40 • €€*) is a good place to try regional food.

■ The Úbeda potters are all located along Calle Valencia; look for the workshops of the premier ceramists, the Tito family.

# TOP 10 ⭐ Parque Nacional de Doñana

Established in 1969, the Parque Nacional de Doñana is an important wetland reserve and a prime site for migrating birds. It covers more than 2,470 sq km (954 sq miles) and its wide variety of ecosystems, rare fauna and abundance of bird life are so vital to the overall environmental stability of Western Europe that it is designated a UNESCO Biosphere Reserve. It yields up its natural wonders gradually, but a trip to western Andalucía is not complete without a visit here.

### ① Setting and History
Located at the estuary of the Guadalquivir River, the area probably owes its present pristine condition to the fact that it was set aside as a hunting preserve for the nobility in the 16th century.

### ④ Habitats
The park features three distinct kinds of ecosystem: dunes **(left)**, *coto* (pine and cork forests and scrubland) and *marisma* (wetlands), which in turn comprise marshes, salt marshes, lagoons and floodplains.

### ② Guided Tours
All-terrain vehicles depart from the Visitor Centres twice daily with itineraries dependent on the time of year. The marshes dry up in the summer months, limiting birdwatching, but this increases the chance of seeing rare mammals.

### ⑤ Fauna
The endangered pardel lynx **(right)** is the emblem of the park. At least 300,000 birds make their home here, among them the flamingo and the purple gallinule, and around 25 pairs of the very rare Iberian eagle also survive here.

**White storks fly over Doñana's wetlands**

### ③ El Rocío's Romería
This town **(below)** is the focal point of one of Spain's largest festivals, the Romería del Rocío. The four-day pilgrimage leading up to Whitsun winds its way through the park. Thousands honour the Virgin of El Rocío (see p80).

### ⑥ Visitor Centres
Several Visitor Centres offer exhibitions as well as planned trails, with rest areas and birdwatching options.

## Flora 7

Umbrella pines and cork-oaks flourish here and both types of tree provide crucial nesting sites for birds. Wild flowers in the dunes and scrubland areas include the bright pink spiny-leafed thrift **(right)**, besom heath, yellow gorse and the bubil lily.

### ECOLOGICAL ISSUES

Despite vigilant efforts to protect the park, in 1998 a Río Tinto mining toxic waste storage reservoir burst, dumping pollutants into the Guadiamar River, one of the wetlands' main tributaries. Thankfully, the poisonous wave of acids and heavy metals was stopped just short of the park, but damage was done to its border areas. As a result of this disaster, strict measures are enforced to prevent further pollution.

## Bird Shelter 10

The Centro de Visitantes El Acebuche, the main visitor centre, is set on a lagoon. At the eastern end there is an aviary where rescued and recuperating birds receive intensive care. It's an opportunity for visitors to view some unusual species.

## El Palacio de Acebrón 8

This Neo-Classical style hunting lodge, built in 1961, has an exhibition on the history and ethno-graphy of the region, and offers good views upstairs. It is a starting point for a 12-km (8-mile) woodland trail nearby.

## Huts 9

Dating from the 18th century, these traditional huts **(right)** are found in the *pinares* (pine forests). Sometimes clustered into small villages, the uninhabited structures are made of pine frames covered with local thatch.

### NEED TO KNOW

**MAP B4** ■ Reservations for 4x4 guided tours 959 43 04 32 ■ 7:30am–7pm daily (to 9pm in summer); tours 8:30am & 5pm (summer), 8:30am & 3pm (winter).

Tours €30

*El Rocío Turismo:* Avda de la Canaliega. 959 44 38 08

*Centro de Visitantes El Acebuche:* Ctra A483, 22 km (14 miles) from Matalascañas. 959 43 96 29

*Centro de Información La Rocina:* 959 43 95 69. Winter: 9am–7pm daily; summer: 10am–3pm & 4–6pm

■ The main visitor centre has a snack bar.

■ Bring binoculars, mosquito repellent, sunscreen and walking shoes – watch out for quicksand.

■ If you join in the Romería del Rocío, you will need a sleeping bag and food.

# TOP 10 ⭐ The Sierra Nevada

The Sierra Nevada ("Snowy Mountains") include Spain's tallest peaks and are Europe's second-highest mountain range after the Alps. Until the 20th century, their only regular visitors were the so-called *neveros* (icemen), who brought back blocks of ice to sell in nearby Granada, and for years the only part the mountains played in a tour of the region was as the glistening backdrop to the Alhambra *(see pp12–13)*. They have now become popular in their own right – for trekking, skiing and exploring the remarkable collection of villages on their southern slopes, Las Alpujarras. The area was made a national park in 1999.

### 1 Setting
Spain's highest peak, the Mulhacén (3,482 m/11,425 ft), is at the western end of the range **(right)**. To the south are fertile valleys.

### 2 Flora and Fauna
Snowcapped most of the year, these heights are still rich in wild-flowers. Some 60 varieties are unique here, such as a giant honeysuckle. Fauna include the ibex and the golden eagle.

### 3 Puerto del Suspiro del Moro
Heading south from Granada on the N323, you'll come to the spot known as the "Pass of the Moor's Sigh". Here, the bereft Boabdil (the last Moorish ruler in Spain), expelled by the Christians, is said to have looked back on his beloved city for the last time.

### 4 Barranco de Poqueira
This vast and gorgeous ravine is home to a stunning collection of tiny villages. Much loved by visitors seeking tranquillity, the remote site even has its own Tibetan Monastery, founded in 1982. The ravine is an excellent place for easy day walks, and each town offers traditional local crafts.

### 5 Las Alpujarras
The southern side of the Sierra Nevada is a dramatic zone, home to a stunning series of white villages **(left)**. The architecture here is pure Moorish, almost identical to that found in the Rif Mountains of Morocco. Houses are flat-roofed, clustered together and joined by little bridges.

### 8 Skiing
The main ski resort, Sol y Nieve (which means "sun and snow"), is Europe's most southerly, and in operation from December to April or even May. The pistes and facilities **(left)** are good enough to have hosted the world Alpine skiing championships.

### 9 Valle de Lecrín
This bucolic valley is filled with almond, olive and citrus groves – the almond blossom is stunning in late winter.

### 10 Hiking
There is a paved road over the top of the range but the uppermost reaches have been closed to cars since the national park was established in January 1999. In summer it's a hiker's paradise **(right)** – the second-highest peak, Veleta (3,470 m/11,385 ft), is a relatively easy 5-hour round trip.

**BRENAN'S SOUTH FROM GRANADA**

In the 1920s, British writer Gerald Brenan, a member of the Bloomsbury set, came to live in the village of Yegen in the eastern Alpujarras. A plaque in the town marks the house he lived in. He noted his experiences in his book *South from Granada*, a wonderful evocation of the place and its people, whose way of life is still largely unchanged. The 2002 Spanish film *Al Sur de Granada*, based on the book, is a delightful dramatization.

### 6 Órgiva
Made the regional capital in 1839, this town remains the area's largest. It's at its best on Thursday mornings, when everyone comes alive for market day, and you can find traditional local products **(above)**.

### 7 Lanjarón
Famous since Roman times for its mineral springs, the town is now a modern *balneario* (spa) and marks the beginning of the Alpujarras proper. Below the main street is a Moorish castle with great views over the gorge.

**NEED TO KNOW**

**MAP F4** ■ Parque Nacional de la Sierra Nevada ■ Ctra Antigua de Sierra Nevada, km 7 ■ 958 98 02 38 ■ www.redde parquesnacionales.mma.es (in Spanish)

*Sierra Nevada Club* (skiing): Plaza de Andalucía 4, Sol y Nieve. 902 70 80 90. www. sierranevada.es

■ Lovers of *jamón serrano* (mountain ham) must not fail to try the delicious snow-cured version that originates from the town of Trevélez.

■ Extra sun protection is vital here, particularly for skiers. Hikers and trekkers should have good walking shoes, something to wear against the wind, water, some food and binoculars.

■ Petrol stations are a rarity in Las Alpujarras. Coming from the west, Órgiva is a good place to fill up.

# The Top 10 of Everything

**Patio de las Doncellas (Courtyard of the Maidens), Real Alcázar, Seville**

# Moments in History

## 1 Bronze Age Developments

The Iberian (Tartessian) civilization developed when bronze began to be smelted and worked in Andalucía around 2500 BC. Some early tribes built the oldest megalithic tombs (*dolmens*) in western Europe.

## 2 Phoenician and Greek colonies

Attracted by the area's mineral wealth, the Phoenicians founded a trading post in around 1100 BC at what is now Cádiz, while the Greeks established a toehold near Málaga in 636 BC. The two maintained a mercantile rivalry until Carthage, a former Phoenician colony, dominated the region.

## 3 Roman Spain

The first Roman town in Spain, Itálica (*see p97*), was established in 206 BC; Rome finally wrested the entire region from the Carthaginians in 201 BC. Due to abundant local produce, Andalucía became one of the empire's wealthiest outposts.

## 4 Arab Domination

Some 700 years later, when the Roman Empire began to come apart, tribes from northern Europe laid claim to the peninsula. The Vandals and then the Visigoths ruled for some three centuries. Political instability and conflict over rightful succession in AD 710 led to the enlistment of Muslim armies from North Africa. The Moors saw their chance and within 10 years they had taken over.

## 5 Moorish Sophistication

The Moors were custodians of the best features of Roman civilization: religious tolerance, scientific and philosophical thought, engineering and art (*see pp44–5*). In the 10th century, Córdoba became the largest and wealthiest city in Europe under the Caliphate of Abd ar-Rahman III.

**Moorish La Mezquita, Córdoba**

## 6 Reconquista

The dissolution of the Caliphate in 1031 marked the beginning of the end for Moorish Spain. Some 30 *taifas* (principalities), jostling for political hegemony, proved no contest for the Christians. The eight-month siege and *reconquista* of Granada in 1492 was the most poignant loss.

**Itálica's Roman amphitheatre**

**Columbus sets sail for the New World**

### 7 Discovery of America
That same year the New World was discovered for Spain by Christopher Columbus. The result was a wealth of gold and silver from the new empire.

### 8 Imperial Collapse
Colonial losses that began in 1713 following the War of Spanish Succession reached their *dénouement* with Spain's defeat in the Spanish-American War of 1898. In Andalucía this long decline meant grinding poverty and mass emigration.

### 9 Franco and the Civil War
The Spanish Civil War (1936–9) was ignited by a military coup led by General Francisco Franco. On 18 July 1936 the war began when Nationalists took Cádiz, Seville and Granada. Then followed the grim years (1939–75) of Franco's dictatorship.

**General Francisco Franco**

### 10 Seville Expo '92
The World's Fair in 1992 celebrated the quincentenary of Columbus's discovery of the New World. It brought 42.5 million visitors and a sprucing up of Seville, but left bankruptcy in its wake. The economic disaster also had a political impact; charges of corruption loosened the Socialist Party's hold on power.

**TOP 10 HISTORIC ANDALUCIAN FIGURES**

**1 Melkarth**
The Phoenician's name for Hercules, whom legend claims to have founded Andalucía.

**2 Trajan**
One of the greatest Roman emperors (AD 98–117) was a native of Itálica.

**3 Hadrian**
Emperor Trajan's successor (AD 117–38) was a great builder, emphasizing Rome's Classical Greek roots.

**4 Abd ar-Rahman III**
The Syrian Emir (AD 912–61) established al-Andalus, an autonomous caliphate.

**5 Boabdil**
The final Moorish ruler (r.1482–92) lost Granada to the Catholic Monarchs.

**6 Isabel and Fernando**
Isabel of Castilla and Fernando of Aragón (1479–1516) were dubbed "The Catholic Monarchs".

**7 Christopher Columbus**
The Genoese sea captain (1451–1506) set sail from Huelva Province and, on 12 October 1492, landed on one of the islands in the Bahamas.

**8 Emperor Carlos V**
His reign (1516–56) left Spain nearly bankrupt, but with cultural legacies such as his palace in Granada *(see p12)*.

**9 Felipe V**
Felipe V (1700–46) had his court in Seville until a claim to the throne by Archduke Charles of Austria led to the War of Spanish Succession.

**10 Felipe González**
A native of Seville, this left-wing leader (1982–96) brought rapid change to Spain and to Andalucía.

**Boabdil at the Alhambra, 1492**

# TOP10 Aspects of Moorish Heritage

### 1 Religious Tolerance
Although non-Muslims had to pay a special tax and wear distinctive clothing, Moorish policies towards Jews and Catholics were generally easy-going. There was greater repression after the fundamentalist Almohads came into power in the 12th century, but on the whole, the various faiths were well integrated for many centuries.

### 2 Music
The Moors can be credited with the early development of the guitar, which they adapted from the four-stringed lute. The Middle Eastern musical forms they imported were also to have an effect later on flamenco (see pp46–7).

### 3 Gardens
Moorish gardens make prominent use of water – so important to people from a perpetually arid land. It was sprayed, channelled, made to gurgle and fall, to please the ear and eye. Jasmine, honey-suckle and roses are just a few of the many flowers the Moors brought to the region.

### 4 Philosophy
Great minds of Andalucía, such as the Moor Averroës and the Jew Maimonides, were considered among the most advanced thinkers of their age. The former almost single-handedly preserved the writings of Aristotle, while the latter's writings sought to reconcile Biblical faith and reason.

**Moses Maimonides**

### 5 Crafts
The hand-tooled leather of Córdoba, silver and gold filigree jewellery, pottery, silk and embroidered goods and inlaid creations all owe their existence to the Moors' 800-year rule.

### 6 Agriculture
Inheriting many of their techniques from the Romans, the Moors were masters of agricultural engineering. Their system consisted of three main elements: the aqueduct, the waterwheel and the irrigation channel. Thereby, they were able to cultivate vast areas, often building ingenious terracing on slopes. They also introduced many crops, including bitter oranges, lemons, almonds, rice, cotton, asparagus and mulberry trees (to feed silk-worms).

**The Partal gardens at the Alhambra**

**Moorish calligraphy, the Alhambra**

### 7 Art and Architecture

Moorish art and architecture is full of signs and symbols and often incorporates calligraphy into its designs, quoting the Koran or poetry. The point was to inspire viewers to reflect upon the unity of all things under Allah, whose power and perfection could never be equalled by the achievements of man.

### 8 Science

Moorish scientists excelled in the fields of metallurgy, zoology, botany, medicine and mathematics. Moorish inventors also developed revolutionary devices such as the astrolabe and the quadrant, both used for navigation. Arabic numerals were introduced, as well as algebra (from *al-jebr*, meaning "reuniting broken parts") and the algorithm.

**A brass astrolabe**

### 9 Food

The simple fare that had existed prior to the Moorish incursion – centred around olives, wheat and grapes – gave way to flavours such as almonds, saffron, nutmeg, pepper and other spices.

### 10 Language

Modern Spanish is full of everyday terms that come from Moorish heritage – the word for "left" (*izquierda*) is almost pure Arabic, as is any word beginning with the prefix *al-* (the).

**TOP 10 MOORISH SITES**

**1 Moorish Granada**
The spectacular Alhambra palace is the gem of Spain's Moorish heritage, while the adjacent Generalife offers sumptuous gardens (see pp12–15).

**2 Real Alcázar, Seville**
The front towers and gateway of Seville's royal palace retain their Moorish origins (see pp20–21).

**3 La Mezquita, Córdoba**
This vast mosque marked the beginning of the Arab-Hispanic style known as Caliphal (see pp24–5).

**4 Baños Árabes, Ronda**
These Moorish baths feature horseshoe arches, typical of Arabic architecture (see p30).

**5 Medina Azahara, Córdoba**
Sadly now in ruins, this once splendid palace epitomized the city's glory in the 10th century (see p125).

**6 Almonaster la Real**
This village's mosque is one of Andalucía's finest, with great views from the minaret (see p98).

**7 Alcazaba, Almería**
One of the largest surviving Moorish fortresses in the region (see p119).

**8 Alcazaba, Málaga**
Remains of the original Moorish walls and tower can still be seen (see p104).

**9 Las Alpujarras**
The villages on the slopes of the Sierra Nevada retain distinctive Moorish architecture (see pp38–9).

**10 Vejer de la Frontera**
The most Moorish of the *pueblos blancos* (see p57).

**Moorish tiling, Real Alcázar**

# TOP10 Aspects of Gypsy Culture

**Women performing Sevillanas, which has its roots in gypsy culture**

### 1 Origins
Gypsies (Roma) arrived in Eastern Europe in the 14th century and in Andalucía in the 15th century. Linguistic research shows that their language, Romany, was related to ancient dialects from northern India. Why they left India is unclear, but it was possibly to escape conflict with invading Muslims.

### 2 Cave-dwellings
In remote hills and mountains, gypsies escaped Christian persecution by turning caves into homes. Although flooding and other natural mishaps have crushed these communities and forced many out, some gypsies return to their former dwellings to perform lively flamenco shows for visitors.

**Inside a cave-dwelling**

### 3 Dance
Similarities between Middle Eastern and North African dance forms and flamenco are obvious. But using the feet to create rapid staccato rhythms, combined with expressive arm and hand gestures, clearly resembles traditional kathak dancing from northern India, revealing flamenco's true roots.

### 4 Song
Despite some persecution in Andalucía, many gypsies stayed, and developed a unique strain of music, flamenco, which draws on Arabic, Jewish and Byzantine sources, as well as their own Indian traditions. Similar to the American Blues, it is the raucous, rhythmic music of the dispossessed and marginalized, full of pathos and catharsis. The word flamenco is probably a corruption of the Arabic *felag mengu* (fugitive peasant).

### 5 Guitar
The six-stringed flamenco guitar can be traced back to the medieval lute. It is lighter, shallower and less resonant than a classical guitar, and can be played extremely fast. A plate below the sound hole is used for tapping out rhythms.

**Flamenco Legends**
A few of the names who advanced the art include: singers El Fillo and La Niña de los Peines; guitarist Paco de Lucía; and dancers La Macarrona and Carmen Amaya.

 **Sevillanas**
This strident dance, with clapping rhythms, has been infused with the flamenco spirit. It is danced with enthusiasm at festivals.

**Horses**
Andalucian gypsies have a reputation for their ability to train their steeds. To watch a gypsy horseman putting an animal through its paces is to witness an amazing display of communication between man and beast.

Riders at the April Fair, Seville

 **History**
Although gypsies have remained outsiders throughout their history, they found a more congenial civilization in Andalucía than anywhere else. The culture was decidedly Middle Eastern and not dissimilar to that of their native land. With the Christian reconquest, however, "pagan" gypsies were forced into hiding or to continue their wanderings.

**Performances**
Historically, flamenco is an improvised performance that arises spontaneously from a gathering, but the rule these days tends towards scheduled spectacles. Still, if the mood is right, these events still generate a great deal of emotion.

**TOP 10 FLAMENCO VENUES**

Performers at El Arenal, Seville

**1 La Taberna Flamenca, Jerez**
MAP B5 ▪ Calle Angostillo de Santiago 3 ▪ 956 32 36 93
Flamboyant shows.

**2 Peña La Bulería, Jerez**
MAP B5 ▪ C/Empedrada 20
▪ 856 05 37 72
Club named after a fast flamenco style that originated in Jerez.

**3 Sanlúcar de Barrameda**
MAP B5
This town holds the Feria de Flamenco festival in July.

**4 Juan Villar, Cádiz**
MAP B5 ▪ Paseo Fernando Quiñones
▪ 956 22 52 90 ▪ Open Tue–Sun (performances Fri)
A good peña for genuine flamenco.

**5 Tablao El Arenal, Seville**
MAP L4 ▪ C/Rodo 7 ▪ 954 21 64 92
First-class performances.

**6 Casa de la Memoria, Seville**
A museum, gallery and cultural centre with performances (see p91).

**7 Tablao Flamenco Cardenal, Córdoba**
MAP D3 ▪ Calle Buen Pastor 2
▪ 691 21 79 22 ▪ Open Mon–Sat
Authentic shows.

**8 Venta El Gallo, Granada**
MAP F4 ▪ Barranco de los Negros 5
▪ 958 22 84 76
Professional performances.

**9 La Peña Platería, Granada**
MAP F4 ▪ Placeta de Toqueros 7
▪ 958 21 06 50
One of Spain's oldest peñas.
Performances Thu and Sat.

**10 Peña El Taranto, Almería**
MAP G4 ▪ C/Tenor Iribarne 20
▪ 950 23 50 57
Named after the dance, the taranto.

# 🔟 Art and Culture

**1  Andrés de Vandelvira**
Andrés de Vandelvira (1509–75) was the quintessential architect of the Spanish Renaissance in Andalucía. His work spanned the three major phases of the style's predominance, from ornamental Plateresque, to Italianate Classical, to austere Herrerean. He can be given virtually sole credit for the architectural treasures in the town of Úbeda and many important edifices in Baeza (see pp34–5).

**2  Francisco de Zurbarán**
The great painter (1598–1664) spent most of his life in and around Seville, where his art adorns many churches and museums. His works are noted for their mystical qualities, dramatized by striking *chiaroscuro* (light and shade) effects.

*A King of Spain* (c. 1645) by Cano

*The Apparition of Saint Peter to Saint Peter Nolasco* (1629) by Zurbarán

**3  Velázquez**
Born in Seville, Diego Rodríguez de Silva y Velázquez (1599–1660) left for Madrid in 1623 to become court painter to the king. His was the most remarkable talent of the golden age of Spanish painting, taking naturalism and technique to new heights. The works that remain in his home town were mostly religious commissions; his real genius lay in portraits.

**Diego Velázquez**

**4  Alonso Cano**
Most of the works created by Alonso Cano (1601–67) can be seen in Granada, largely because after he was accused of killing his wife the city vowed to protect him if he would work exclusively for them. Sadly, such a predicament limited the opportunities for this gifted painter, sculptor and architect to blossom to his full potential.

**5  Murillo**
Bartolomé Esteban Murillo (1618–82) was the most successful of the Baroque painters from Seville. He received countless commissions to produce devotional works, notably the many *Immaculate Conceptions* seen in Andalucía.

**6  Pedro Roldán**
Roldán (1624–99) was one of the chief proponents of the Spanish aspiration to combine painting, sculpture and architecture into unified works of art, such as the altarpiece in Seville's Hospital de la Caridad (see p88).

**Palacio de San Telmo, Seville**

### 7 Leonardo de Figueroa

Figueroa (1650–1730) was an accomplished Baroque architect. His commissions in Seville included the Palacio de San Telmo, the Hospital de los Venerables *(see p88)* and the Museo de Bellas Artes *(see p87)*.

### 8 Manuel de Falla

Andalucian-born de Falla (1876– 1946) was Spain's finest classical composer. One of his major works, *The Three-Cornered Hat*, has its roots deep in flamenco.

### 9 Picasso

Pablo Picasso (1881–1973) was born in Málaga, although he settled in France in 1909. His native land, with images of the bullfight and later of the horrors of the Franco era, featured in his work throughout his career.

**Statue of Picasso, Málaga**

### 10 Federico García Lorca

The Granada-born poet and playwright (1898–1936) was also an artist, musician, theatre director and more. Homosexual and Socialist too, he was murdered by Franco's Nationalists at the start of the Spanish Civil War. His work shows his love for Andalucian culture.

## TOP 10 WORKS INSPIRED BY ANDALUCÍA

**1 Lord Byron**
The English Romantic poet's fascination with Andalucía is chronicled in his *Don Juan* (1819).

**2 Michael Jacobs**
*Factory of Light* (2003) is a vivid, witty and informative account of life in the Andalucian village of Frailes, near Jaén.

**3 Washington Irving**
The American writer lived in Granada for some time and produced the hit *Tales of the Alhambra* (1832).

**4 Chris Stewart**
Former Genesis drummer wrote the funny and insightful *Driving Over Lemons*, a memoir about relocating to an Andalucian farmhouse.

**5 Serafín Estébanez Calderón**
This Málaga-born writer's *Andalucian Scenes* (1847) featured the first literary description of a gypsy festival.

**6 Opera**
Operas set in Andalucía include *The Marriage of Figaro* (1786, Mozart), *The Barber of Seville* (1816, Rossini) and *Carmen* (1875, Bizet).

**7 Manuel Machado**
The works of Machado (1874–1947), such as *Cante Jondo*, evoke a poetic passion for Andalucía.

**8 Dalí and Buñuel**
This Surrealist pair created the avant garde film *Un Chien d'Andalou* in 1928.

**9 Ernest Hemingway**
*For Whom the Bell Tolls* (1940) was based on the American writer's Andalucian experiences during Spain's Civil War.

**10 Salman Rushdie**
The British Indian author's *The Moor's Last Sigh* (1995) was inspired by the exile of Granada's last Moorish king.

**Scene from *The Barber of Seville***

# 🔟 Alcázares, Palacios and Castillos

**1** **Real Alcázar, Seville**
This sumptuous palace and extensive gardens constitute a world of royal luxury. The architectural styles are a blend of mainly Moorish traditions – note the lavish use of the horseshoe arch, glazed tilework and wood ceilings *(see pp20–21)*.

**2** **Palacio de las Dueñas, Seville**
**MAP M1** ■ C/Dueñas 5 ■ Open 10am– 6pm Mon–Thu (to 3pm Fri) ■ Adm
Built between the 15th and 16th centuries, this luxurious palace is the official city residence of the Duke of Alba. In addition to its magnificent architecture, which is a combination of Gothic and Moorish styles, one of the main attractions of Las Dueñas is its vast collection of art.

**3** **Fortaleza de la Mota, Alcalá la Real**
This Moorish castle, crowning the hill above the town, is the chief attraction here. Created by Granada's rulers in the 14th century, it incorporates 12th-century structures and earlier elements, since the strategically situated town dates from prehistoric times. After the Christian reconquest in 1341 *(see p42)*, additions to the fortress continued till the 16th century. The keep houses a "Life on the Frontier" visitor centre.

**Fortaleza de la Mota, Alcalá la Real**

**Decorative tiles, La Casa de Pilatos**

**4** **Casa de Pilatos, Seville**
Few palaces are more opulent than this 16th-century mansion. A mix of Mudéjar (Christian-Islamic), flamboyant Gothic and Renaissance styles, it is adorned with Classical sculptures, including a 5th-century BC Greek Athena and important Roman works. A noble residence to this day, it is filled with family portraits and antiques *(see p85)*.

**5** **Palacio del Marqués de la Gomera, Osuna**
**MAP D4** ■ C/San Pedro 20 ■ 954 81 22 23
Now a hotel and restaurant, this 18th-century palace is a striking example of the Spanish Baroque style. The family escutcheon crowns the carved stone doorway.

**Palacio de Jabalquinto, Baeza**

### 6 Palacio de Jabalquinto, Baeza

This 15th-century palace is a study in originality. The façade defies categorization, while the gallery and the patio evoke the Renaissance style. The latter has a Baroque staircase *(see p34)*.

### 7 Castillo de Santa Catalina, Jaén

MAP F3 ▪ 953 12 07 33 ▪ Open mid-May–mid-Sep: 10am–2pm & 5–9pm Mon–Sat, 10am–3pm Sun; mid-Sep–mid-May: 10am–6pm Mon–Sat (to 3pm Sun) ▪ Adm

Restored by the Christians, this 13th-century castle towers above the town and affords spectacular views.

### 8 Castillo de Burgalimar, Baños de la Encina

MAP F2 ▪ Cerro del Cueto, Plaza de Santa María 1 ▪ Visit by appt, 953 61 33 38 ▪ Adm

This Moorish castle is one of the best-preserved in Andalucía. Its horseshoe-arched main gate bears an inscription dating its construction to AD 967. Some 14 square towers provide vistas far and wide.

### 9 Castillo de La Calahorra

MAP F4 ▪ 958 67 70 98 ▪ Open 10am–1pm, 4–6pm Wed ▪ Adm

One of the few castles built after the Christian reconquest, this was also one of the first in Spain to be built in Italian Renaissance style. Despite its forbidding situation and exterior, its inner courtyard is exquisite.

**Castillo de Vélez Blanco**

### 10 Castillo de Vélez Blanco

MAP H3 ▪ 607 41 50 55 ▪ Open 10am–2pm & 4–6pm (Apr–Sep: 5–8pm) Wed–Sun

This has the grace of a fairy-tale castle. Unfortunately, it was gutted in the early 1900s, but a reconstruction of one of the patios gives you some idea of its original splendour.

# 🔟 Places of Worship

### 1 Mosque, Almonaster la Real

MAP B3 ■ Ayuntamiento ■ 959 14 30 03 ■ Open 9am–8pm daily

Virtually unchanged for 1,000 years, this is one of Andalucía's few surviving rural mosques. Inside, it has the oldest *mihrab* (Mecca-facing prayer niche) in Spain *(see p98)*.

**Mosque, Almonaster la Real**

### 2 La Colegiata de la Asunción, Osuna

From its hilltop, this massive Spanish Renaissance church dominates the town. Its austere façade is relieved by a fine Plateresque portal, the Puerta del Sol. Inside, treasures include five masterpieces by José de Ribera, a Crucifixion sculpture by Juan de Mesa, beautiful Renaissance ornamentation and a wonderful Baroque altarpiece *(see p96)*.

### 3 Oratorio de San Felipe Neri, Cádiz

MAP B5 ■ Plaza San Felipe Neri ■ 662 64 22 33 ■ Open 10:30am–2pm & 4:30–8pm Tue–Fri, 10:30am–2pm Sat, 10am–1pm Sun ■ Adm

As the commemorative plaques adorning the façade reveal, this fine Baroque church is one of the most significant buildings in Spain. On 29 March 1812, Spanish patriots defied a Napoleonic blockade and met here to compose the country's first constitution. The document's liberal ideas have inspired fledgling democracies ever since.

### 4 Monasterio de San Jerónimo, Granada

MAP F4 ■ C/Rector López Argueta 9 ■ 958 27 93 37 ■ Open Mar–Aug: 10am–1:30pm & 4–7:30pm daily; Sep–Feb: 10am–1pm & 3–6:30pm Mon–Sat ■ Adm

This Renaissance magnum opus is largely the creation of Diego de Siloé, one of the great masters of the age. The façade's upper window is flanked by sinuous mythological animals and medallions. The altar is complex and monumental, consisting of row upon row of high reliefs framed by columns.

**Monasterio de San Jerónimo, Granada**

**Moorish arches inside La Mezquita**

## 5 La Mezquita, Córdoba
This spectacular mosque may have been savagely reconsecrated but visitors can still see its Byzantine mosaics and other exquisite marvels *(see pp24–5)*.

## 6 Iglesia de San Mateo, Lucena
**MAP E3** ■ **Open during services**
It's intriguing to find one of the masterpieces of Andalucian Rococo design in this industrial town – Lucena was famous for having been a virtually independent Jewish enclave during Moorish rule. The gem of this 15th-century church is its 18th-century octagonal sacristy and the complex decoration of the chapel and its dome.

## 7 Catedral de Jaén
The cathedral was primarily the work of famed Renaissance architect Andrés de Vandelvira, although the west façade was designed later, decorated with Baroque sculptures by Pedro Roldán. Each Friday, at 10:30am–noon and 5–6pm, one of Spain's holiest relics, the Reliquía del Santo Rostro de Cristo, is brought out for the faithful to kiss. This is believed to be the cloth that St Veronica used to wipe Christ's face on the road to Calvary. A miraculous impression of the holy face is said to have been left upon it *(see p127)*.

## 8 Seville Cathedral
The vast cathedral is Seville's most striking architectural masterpiece. It has soaring columns, precious artworks and the world's largest altarpiece *(see pp18–19)*.

## 9 Capilla Real and Catedral, Granada
Although not without aesthetic merit, these two structures are more about Christian triumph and royal ego than they are about spirituality. At the Royal Chapel's sarcophagi, note how Queen Isabel's head presses more deeply into her marble pillow than that of King Fernando – said to indicate greater intelligence. In the cathedral is the equestrian statue *El Matamoros* ("The Killer of Moors") by Alonso de Mena *(see pp116–7)*.

**Granada cathedral's lavish interior**

## 10 Çapilla del Salvador, Ubeda
Designed by Siloé and Vandelvira, this masterpiece of Andalucian Renaissance was commissioned as a family pantheon and is still privately owned. The sacristy is the highlight, employing caryatids and atlantes as columns and pilasters. It was once embellished by a Michelangelo sculpture, a sad casualty of the Spanish Civil War *(see p35)*.

# ⭐🔟 **Museums and Galleries**

### ① Museo Arqueológico Antiquarium, Seville

**MAP M2** ▪ Plaza de la Encarnación ▪ 955 47 15 80 ▪ Open 10am–8pm Tue–Sat, 10am–2pm Sun and public hols ▪ Adm

This subterranean museum, situated below the extraordinary Metropol Parasol structure in Plaza de la Encarnación, showcases the fascinating archaeological remains found in 1973 when the Parasol complex was being built. Extensive Roman ruins date from the Tiberius era onwards (around 30–600 AD) and there is a Moorish house dating back to the 12th–13th century.

### ② Museo de Bellas Artes, Seville

Housed in an exquisite former convent, this art museum is second only to Madrid's famed Prado. Paintings include early works by Velasquez, and important pieces by Zurbarán, Ribera, El Greco, Murillo, Valdés Leal and Vásquez *(see p87)*.

**Museo de Bellas Artes, Seville**

### ③ Museo del Bandolero, Ronda

This offbeat museum celebrates the story and legend of the Serranía's famous bandits and highwaymen. Mostly active in the 19th century, they captured the imagination of many writers of the period, who portrayed them as romantic figures living a devil-may-care life in communion with nature. As the exhibits here will attest, they were anything but "diamonds in the rough" *(see p31)*.

**Exhibit at the Museo del Bandolero**

### ④ Museo Picasso, Málaga

This is the world's third-largest museum dedicated to the modern master, and honours Picasso's wish for his native city to have a part of his artistic legacy. With over 187 paintings, including some major canvases, the museum collection covers eight decades of the artist's career and gives an idea of the breadth and depth of Picasso's work *(see p104)*.

### ⑤ Archivo General de Indias, La Lonja, Seville

This museum is a vast archive given over to the discovery and conquest of the New World; four centuries of Spanish empire are painstakingly catalogued. The museum is housed in an 18th- century edifice that was built as the merchants' exchange *(see p78)*. The building and the archive are registered as a World Heritage Site by UNESCO.

**Journey Through the Human Body exhibition, Museo Parque de las Ciencias**

### 6 Museo Parque de las Ciencias, Granada

This dazzling science park is home to a range of interactive exhibitions on such topics as the human body, outer space, the environment and technology *(see p118)*.

### 7 Museo Municipal, Antequera

This museum is located in a striking 18th-century ducal palace, which means that many of the exhibits simply cannot compete with the context. Two that do, however, are the life-size 1st-century AD Roman bronze representing a naked young man, possibly Ganymede, cupbearer to the gods, and a life-like carving of St Francis of Assisi in wood by Pedro de Mena, a 17th-century Andalucian master *(see p104)*.

### 8 Museo de Cádiz

A Neo-Classical mansion houses Cádiz's main museum, a rich mix of archaeological treasures and fine art. The museum features arti-facts from the city's ancient cultures, including jewellery, pottery and small bronzes, but most notably a pair of 5th-century BC marble sarcophagi. Among the art are works by Zurbarán, Rubens, Murillo and Cano. An ethnological collection features pieces that highlight aspects of the city's culture *(see p27)*.

### 9 Museo Arqueológico, Córdoba

A small 16th-century Renaissance mansion is home to this excellent collection, highlighting the city's importance in Roman times. In fact, the mansion was built over a Roman structure and there is an ancient patio to prove it. A sculpture of the Persian god Mithras, found at Cabra, is particularly fine. Other parts of the collection focus on Iberian finds and Moorish artifacts *(see p23)*.

**Patio of the Museo Arqueológico**

### 10 Museo Provincial de Jaén

The lower floor contains some truly extraordinary 5th-century BC Iberian stone sculptures. Found near the town of Porcuna, in the western part of the province, they show clear influences from Greek works. Upstairs, the museum has some fine medieval wood sculpture *(see p127)*.

# ▤⑩ Villages

 **Almonaster la Real**

From a distance, this lovely *pueblo blanco* in Huelva Province looks like a sprinkling of snow amid the green of the surrounding forests. The citadel features one of the oldest mosques in the region, dating from the 10th century *(see p98)*.

**Monument on the cliff above Alájar**

**② Alájar**

Another pretty Huelva Province village, where the stone houses seem ageless. There are some nice Baroque churches too. More intriguing, however, is the mystical importance of the place, as seen in the hallowed caves and hermitage on the cliff above the town *(see p98)*.

**③ El Rocío**

Deserted for the majority of the year, except for its handful of residents – who still customarily get around on horseback – this town overflows with around one million pilgrims during the annual Romería *(see p36)*. It's worth a visit at any time to take in its wonderful Wild West-style architecture, as well as to book a tour of the nearby Doñana nature reserve *(see pp36–7)*.

 **Cazorla**
MAP G3

Simple whitewashed cubes cluster around a citadel here, while birds of prey overhead remind you that this is the southwestern entrance to the Sierra de Cazorla *(see p61)*. The town's position made it a prize for Moors and Christians, hence the castle in town and the ruined La Iruela, 1 km (0.5 miles) away.

 **Arcos de la Frontera**

The historic part of this town is from the Cuesta de Belén to the Puerta de Matrera – a zone that has been a beautifully preserved national monument since 1962. Central to the area is the Plaza del Cabildo, with ancient walls in evidence and set about with orange trees. Sadly, the castle below the square is not open to the public, but the terrace of the parador opposite is a fine place for a drink with a view *(see p106)*.

**Narrow street in Vejer de la Frontera**

### 6 Vejer de la Frontera

This inland village in Cádiz Province probably retains its quintessential Moorishness more than any other town in Andalucía. It stands gleaming white on a hill with a view of the coast, and its warren of maze-like alleys and byways is virtually indistinguishable from any North African town. Before the Spanish Civil War, women here wore a traditional veiled garment like the Muslim *hijab*, called the *cobijado*; now they are only worn during August festival *(see p107)*.

### 7 Iznatoraf
MAP F2

This mountain eyrie of a place opens out onto 360-degree panoramas of the Cazorla highland. The best view is from the mirador above the cliff at the village's northern edge.

### 8 Zahara de la Sierra
MAP C4

The town's name means "flower" in Arabic and this quiet little hamlet, scented with orange groves, lives up to its reputation. It's a delight to see on the approach and offers fine views once there. The ruined castle, however, stands witness to tougher times. In the 15th century it was attacked continually, sought by both Muslims and Christians for its position guarding the access route to the Serranía de Ronda.

### 9 Sabiote
MAP F2

This hamlet is a hidden gem. It boasts a Roman pedigree, its medieval walls are largely intact, and it has one of the most impressive castles in the region – Moorish in origin but restored by the famed architect Andrés de Vandelvira, who was born here.

**Restored ruins of Sabiote castle**

### 10 Castril
MAP G3

At the foot of an imposing stone outcropping and surrounded by the Parque Natural de la Sierra de Castril, this enchanting town dates back to Roman times. A mountain torrent surges below the idyllic hamlet.

**The approach to Zahara de la Sierra**

# 🔟 Paseos, Plazas, Parks and Gardens

## ① Alcázar de los Reyes Cristianos, Córdoba

MAP D3 ■ Campo Santo de los Mártires ■ 957 42 01 51 ■ Open 8:30am–8:15pm Tue–Fri (to 4pm Sat, 2pm Sun) ■ Adm (free 8:30–9:30am Tue–Fri) ■ www.alcazardelosreyescristianos.cordoba.es

Another of the major delights of Córdoba are the grounds of this palace (see p23). The gardens are lavishly done in Moorish style, indulging in a profusion of colour setting off the sun-bleached stone walls and ancient carvings.

**Alcázar de los Reyes Cristianos**

## ② Plaza San Juan de Dios, Cádiz

MAP B5

This is one of Cádiz's busiest hubs of commercial and social life. Lined with cafés, bars and palm trees, its chief adornment is the monumental Neo-Classical façade of the Ayuntamiento (town hall), along with several handsome towers. The square opens out onto the port, ensuring a constant stream of pedestrians and opportunities for hours of people-watching.

## ③ Parque Genovés, Cádiz

MAP B5

Lying along the west side of Cádiz, this swathe of landscaped greenery facing the seafront has paths for strolling along, some civic sculpture and interesting flora, including an ancient dragon tree originally from the Canary Islands. This is one leg of a two-part park, the other half curving around along the northern seafront.

## ④ Parque Zoológico, Jerez

MAP B5 ■ C/ Madreselva ■ 956 14 97 85 ■ Open 10am–6pm Tue–Sun (May–Sep: 10am–7pm) ■ Adm ■ www.zoobotanicojerez.com

Jerez's small zoo, set in botanical gardens, is also an active centre for the rehabilitation of regional endangered species or any injured animals. The star turns are a pair of white tigers. This is the only chance you may get to see the elusive and extremely rare Iberian lynx, of which only an estimated 1,000 remain in the wild.

## ⑤ Paseo Alcalde Marqués de Contadero, Seville

This central promenade is one of Seville's loveliest. Stretching along the riverfront, within sight of most of the major monuments, its tree-lined walkways make a pleasant break from the crowded city streets. The *paseo* is also pedestrianized so you don't have to worry about traffic as you stroll (see p89).

**Paseo Marqués de Contadero, Seville**

**A pavilion in Parque de María Luisa**

### 6 Jardín Botánico la Concepción, Málaga

MAP E5 ▪ Ctra N331, km 166, Málaga ▪ 951 92 61 79 ▪ Open 9:30am–4:30pm Tue–Sun (Apr–Sep: to 7:30pm) ▪ Adm ▪ www.laconcepcion.malaga.eu

Just north of Málaga lies this impressive botanical garden, the work of a 19th-century English woman, Amalia Livermore, and her Spanish husband, Jorge Loring Oyarzábal. The garden houses a collection of palms and exotic plants from around the world. The grounds are also embellished with charming touches, such as a domed gazebo decorated with tiles and columns. Visitors can stay in the garden for an hour and a half after the closing time.

**Jardín Botánico la Concepción**

### 7 Plaza de la Corredera, Córdoba

MAP D3

Córdoba gave this 17th-century arcaded square a long overdue sprucing up for the tourist onslaught of 1992 (see p43), even putting in an underground car park. But it still retains some of its customary functions, including an open-air market on Saturday morning, in addition to the regular market in the building with the clock tower. The arches provide shade for cafés and tapas bars, from where you can admire the brick façades with wrought-iron balconies.

### 8 Parque de María Luisa, Seville

Seville's glorious main park was a gift to the city from a Bourbon duchess in 1893. It was redesigned for the 1929 Ibero-American Exhibition. Numerous lavish structures have been left behind, including the stunning Plaza de España and several other fine buildings, two of which house local museums. The grounds are largely the creation of Jean-Claude Nicolas Forestier, the French landscape gardener who also designed the Bois de Boulogne in Paris (see p89).

### 9 Plaza Nueva, Granada

MAP Q2

Located at the base of both the Alhambra hill and Albaicín (see pp12–17), and providing views along the banks of the river that runs beneath the city, this is a great place to while away the time. There are street performers, and plenty of cafés with tables outside.

### 10 Paseo de la Constitución, Baeza

MAP F2

Baeza's hub for strollers and café-goers is this oblong central promenade. Fountains grace its tree-lined length, and there are bars with shady seating. Interesting buildings by the square include La Alhóndiga, the former corn exchange (see p34).

# 🔟 Nature Reserves

**Limestone rock formations at El Torcal de Antequera**

### ① El Torcal de Antequera
MAP D4

Málaga Province's most dramatic natural sight is this limestone massif, carved by the weather over countless millennia into bizarre forms. It's a popular destination for hikers and climbers.

### ② Parque Nacional Sierra Nevada

Spain's highest mountains and Europe's southernmost ski resort can be found in this national park. It's a wonderful area for hiking, horse riding and mountain biking (see pp38–9).

### ③ Sierra de Aracena y Picos de Aroche Park

This part of the Sierra Morena in Huelva Province is very rural in character; traditions cling tighter here, notably the culinary techniques that give rise to its world-famous ham, *jamón ibérico*. The forested hills lend themselves to exploration on foot or horseback (see p98).

### ④ Sierra Norte
MAP C3

Sevilla Province's northern reaches are wild and beautiful. Hiking is often a better option than driving, due to rough, pot-holed roads. A great choice for outdoor enthusiasts of any sort – anglers, hunters and climbers are in their element here.

### ⑤ Parque Nacional de Doñana

These important floodplains are a UNESCO Biosphere Reserve and have been a national park since 1969. The ecosystems include sand dunes, pine and cork forests, marshes, scrubland and riverbank. More than six million birds stop here during their migrations and fauna includes the last of the Iberian lynx population (see pp36–7).

### ⑥ Sierra de Grazalema
MAP C5

Some 132,200 acres of verdant wilderness were designated a UNESCO Biosphere Reserve in 1977. Access is strictly controlled and is only possible on foot.

**Walking in the Sierra de Grazalema**

### 7 Cabo de Gata-Níjar
MAP H4

In Almería Province, a stretch of pristine coastline has been set aside as a nature reserve, with towering rocks setting off beaches and coves. The semi-desert massif was designated a UNESCO Biosphere Reserve in 1997. The zone is excellent for scuba-diving (see p65).

### 8 Sierra de Cazorla
MAP G2

In eastern Jaén Province, this vast and enormously diverse park is home to some 1,300 known species of flora, including 20 that are unique to the zone. Steep cliffs, deep gorges and an intricate pattern of rivers, lakes and streams typify the terrain. The area offers plenty of walking opportunities.

Sierra de Cazorla

### 9 Parque Natural de la Sierra de Cardeña y Montoro
MAP E2

This beautiful park is home to forests of holm oak, cork and pine. For the most part gently rolling, it gives way to more dramatic topography in the west. There are plenty of hiking trails and places to spot local fauna.

### 10 Parque Natural de los Montes de Málaga
MAP E5

Most of this park was planted to cloak Málaga's once barren heights so as to prevent the seasonal flooding the city experienced for several centuries. Just 30 minutes from town, it's a fine place for hiking and biking, with colour-coded trails.

---

**TOP 10 FLORA AND FAUNA**

**Flamingoes at Fuente de Piedra**

**1 Trees**
These include black and umbrella pine, holm oak, hazel, olive, citrus, cypress, juniper, ash and the rare Spanish fir.

**2 Shrubs**
Along the coast you'll see agave, brought here from America in the 18th century. Also prickly pear, bullrush, club rush, oleander and arbutus.

**3 Wild flowers**
Look for the Cazorla violet, bubil lily, Nevada daffodil and white celandine.

**4 Raptors**
Birds of prey include the Spanish imperial eagle, the golden eagle and the peregrine falcon.

**5 Songbirds**
Listen out for the red-legged partridge, collared pratincole and hoopoe.

**6 Marsh birds**
Watery areas abound in cranes, flamingoes, wild ducks, gull-billed terns, purple gallinules, stilts, glossy ibis and redshanks.

**7 Mammals**
Wild creatures include wolves, lynxes, boar, genets, civets, mongoose, monk seal, dolphins, whales and the Barbary macaques of Gibraltar.

**8 Reptiles and Amphibians**
This group includes the Montpellier snake, the Spanish lizard and the natterjack toad.

**9 Fish**
Local catch includes black perch, eel, gambusia, tuna, monkfish, sardines, anchovies and cephalopods.

**10 Insects and Arachnids**
Most of Europe's butterflies are found here, along with mosquitoes, scorpions and tarantulas.

*Following pages Hiker, El Torcal de Antequera*

# 🔟 Beaches

**Playa Puerto del Mar, Almuñécar**

## 1 Almuñécar
MAP F5

The main resort on the Costa Tropical of Granada Province is a more relaxed alternative to the intensity of the Costa del Sol. The two central beaches are the Playa San Cristóbal and the Playa Puerto del Mar, separated by a headland. Good diving and windsurfing spots can be found along here *(see p119)*.

## 2 Mazagón
MAP B4

Huelva Province's Costa de la Luz has several appealingly remote beaches, and Mazagón is one of them. Located 23 km (14 miles) southeast of Huelva, this low-key resort is surrounded by pines and has lovely dune beaches. Deserted in winter, it comes alive in summer, mostly with Spanish families, but there's plenty of empty expanse to find solitude.

## 3 Chipiona
MAP B5

Cádiz Province has some good beach resorts that lack the high tourism of further along the coast, and Chipiona is one of the nicest. The beaches are excellent and the town has retained its age-old traditions. It's still a thriving fishing port, for example, as well as a renowned producer of the local sweet muscatel wine. In addition, historic attractions include the longest jetty in the Guadalquivir estuary, known as Turris Caepionis to the Romans and these days as Torre Scipio *(see p107)*.

## 4 Tarifa
MAP C6

Cádiz Province's – and Europe's – southernmost point is one of the best spots in the world for devotees of the West Wind. The wind rarely ceases blowing here, which makes it a top spot for kite- and windsurfing, but less ideal for sunbathers. Still, it is possible to find protected niches that shelter you from the wind, and the nightlife and sense of fun here are second to none *(see p107)*.

**Windsurfing off the beach at Tarifa**

## 5 Marbella
### MAP D5

The Costa del Sol's smartest town naturally has several fine beaches to recommend. To the east there are Cabo Pino, a nudist beach, and Las Dunas, sand dunes beside a modern marina. To the west is a string of party beaches, good for barbecues and dancing, including Victor's Beach and Don Carlos, perhaps Marbella's best (see p32).

**Sierra Blanca mountains, Marbella**

## 6 Torremolinos
### MAP E5

Considering that they are in the main Costa del Sol nightlife magnet, Torremolinos's beaches come as a pleasant surprise. Because of the steep streets, most of the action remains above as you make your way down to the sand (see p33).

## 7 Torre del Mar
### MAP E5

Very much off the beaten Costa del Sol track, this area – frequented mostly by local Spanish families – has quite a bit going for it if you want a more low-key time (see p33).

## 8 Nerja
### MAP E5

This little town is a favourite for those who want an alternative to the brash Costa del Sol. It's a welcoming spot, with a wonderful position on top of an imposing cliff with palm-fringed beaches below (see p33).

## 9 Ayamonte
### MAP A4

Andalucía's westernmost town is located at the mouth of Río Guadiana, and just to the east are the beach resorts Isla Canela and Isla Cristina. Isla Canela has a long, broad beach and an array of bars, while Isla Cristina boasts a fine sandy stretch and a harbour.

## 10 Cabo de Gata
### MAP H5

Almería Province offers some of the finest unspoilt beaches in the region, including the Cala de la Media Luna and the Playa de Mónsul. The main resort town in this natural park is San José (see p61).

**Playa de Mónsul, Cabo de Gata**

# 🔟 Outdoor Activities and Sports

**Horse riding in the Sierra Nevada mountains**

### ① Horse Riding
Far and Ride (4 destinations in Andalucía): MAP C5; 0845 00 66 552 (from UK), +44 1462 701 110 (intnl); www.farandride.com ■ Rutas a Caballo Castellar de la Frontera: C/ Principe Juan Carlos 30; 629 57 24 46; www.castellargp.es

Andalucía is renowned for breeding fine horses and offers a range of riding options, with trails and schools in every province.

### ② Windsurfing and Surfing
ION Club: MAP C6; +49 8819 096 010; www.ion-club.net ■ Windsurf la Herradura: MAP F5; Paseo Marítimo 34; 958 64 01 43; www.windsurflaherradura.com

Tarifa is a magnet for windsurfers, while good possibilities can also be found along the Costa Tropical. For board surfing, the Costa de la Luz

**Windsurfing at Tarifa**

provides sufficiently high waves. Mediterranean waves are only good for body-boarding.

### ③ Hiking
 FEDAMON: 958 29 13 40 ■ www.fedamon.com

Andalucía's sierras, which range from verdant to desert-like and rocky, are perfect for hiking *(see pp60–61)*. If mountaineering appeals, head for the Sierra Nevada. Maps and lists of refuges are available from the Federación Andaluza de Montañismo (FEDAMON).

### ④ Spelunking
MAP D5 ■ Team4you: Centro Commercial Cristamar B64, Puerto Banús, Marbella ■ 952 90 50 82 ■ www.team4you.es

The region has some of the world's most interesting caves, many of them commercially developed. For information and organized jaunts, contact Team4you.

### ⑤ Skiing
Sol y Nieve ski resort near Granada is the only possibility in Andalucía. Although a little too sleek compared to its Alpine cousins, it offers a variety of runs and, best of all, skiing fairly late in the season *(see p39)*.

### ⑥ Boating and Fishing
Spanish Fishing Federation: C/Diego Fernández Herrera 19, 2ª Planta, Puerta B 11401, Jerez de la Frontera (Cádiz); 956 18 75 85; www.fapd.net ■ Spanish Sailing Federation: Avda Libertad, Puerto de Santa María (Cádiz); 956 85 48 13; www.fav.es

With so many marinas along the coast, sailing is big here. For deep-sea and freshwater fishing, you will need to obtain a licence.

### 7 Golf

So copious are the golf courses that the Costa del Sol has often been dubbed the "Costa del Golf". Courses include everything from world masterpieces, designed by top golfers, to putting greens suitable for families *(see p109)*.

### 8 Diving

**Yellow Sub Tarifa: MAP C6; 956 68 06 80; www.divingtarifa.com** ■ **Centro de Buceo Isub: MAP H5; Calle Babor 3, San José de Níjar; 950 38 00 04; www.isubsanjose.com**

Off Gibraltar are many sunken ships, while the wilds around Cabo de Gata offer the most profuse underwater life. The Costa de la Luz also has some good spots, including watersport heaven, Tarifa.

**Diving at Cabo de Gata**

### 9 Fútbol

*Fútbol* (soccer) is a national obsession, stirring up the deepest of passions. In season, you'll encounter it in every bar, blaring out from the TV, along with animated locals.

### 10 Bullfighting

For the Spanish, this is not really a sport, but an art form, and to many Andalucians, it embodies the soul of the region. The fight season runs from April to October and tickets are available from bullrings.

**TOP 10 ASPECTS OF BULLFIGHTING**

**A matador "fighting" a bull**

**1 History**
The bullfight may have roots in primordial religions involving bull sacrifice.

**2 Scheduling**
Despite a slight decline in popularity, about 500 bullfights take place in Spain each year, usually as part of a *feria*.

**3 The Fight**
A bullfight is divided up into three stages called *tercios*. Usually three groups fight two bulls each.

**4 Cast of Characters**
The fight *(corrida)* begins with a procession of all the bullfighters.

**5 Picadores**
In the first *tercio* the matador taunts the bull with a red cape. The *picadors* goad the bull on horseback with steel-pointed lances to weaken the animal's powerful drive.

**6 Banderilleros**
Next the *banderilleros* enter on foot, sticking pairs of spikes in his back, to provoke the bull further into a frenzy.

**7 Matador**
In the final *tercio* the matador makes passes with the *muleta* cape, bringing the fight to its climax.

**8 The Kill**
This should be a quick thrust of the sword, straight to the heart.

**9 Post Mortem**
Matadors are still idolized in Spain, and the crowd cheers when his job is done well and the bull is dragged away.

**10 Celebration**
At the end of a good fight, a band plays, roses are tossed, hankies are waved, and the matador may be carried out on his men's shoulders.

# 🔟 Hikes and Drives

**Walking through the Sierra de Aracena natural park**

### ① Hike from Alájar to Linares de la Sierra
MAP B3

The Sierra de Aracena is defined by soaring cliffs, wooded valleys and whitewashed villages. A good 6-km (4-mile) hike along marked trails leads from Alájar to Linares, via the hamlet of Los Madroñeros. From the main square in Alájar, it follows the old road, with only one steep section.

### ② Hike around the Villages of the Southern Tahá
MAP F4

This hike descends south from Pitres to arrive first at Mecinilla, then along a ravine to Mecina-Fondales. From here, you take the short or long route to Ferreirola, climb up to Atalbéitar and then back to Pitres.

### ③ Hike from Rute to Iznájar
MAP E4

Leave Rute on the A331 south, veer left at the fork and then take the trail on the right about 500 m (550 yd) further on. This leads down to the reservoir; turn right and continue to a rocky promontory. Enjoy the views, then go up the hill and cross the bridge to the scenic village of Iznájar.

### ④ Serranía de Ronda Hike
MAP D5

An easy, picturesque hike connects the village of Benaoján Estación with Jimera de Líbar Estación. Begin at the Molino del Santo hotel, walk down the hill and left alongside the railway and then over it at the second crossing. Across the river is the path; when it divides, take the left fork and continue on Via Pecuaria to town.

### ⑤ Drive from Nerja to Almería
MAP E5 ■ Rte N340

This route takes you along some of the region's most panoramic coast-line. Nerja is built up on cliffs *(see p33)*, and as you approach Almería the views are dramatic *(see p119)*.

### ⑥ Río Borosa Hike
MAP G2

From the visitors' centre at the village of Torre del Vinagre, near Cazorla, this hike takes you along the narrow rock walls of the Cerrada de Elías gorge above the Río Borosa, criss-crossed by wooden bridges.

**Cerrada de Elías gorge**

## 7 Drive from Tarifa to Cádiz

**MAP C6 ■ Rte N340**

With immense cliffs and mammoth sand dunes, this wild sweep of the Costa de la Luz *(see p106)* is the best of the Atlantic shore. The villages of Bolonia, with its ancient Roman sites, and Vejer de la Frontera, which is steeped in Moorish heritage, both make excellent side trips.

## 8 Drive from Ronda to Jerez

**MAP C5 ■ Rte N342**

The attraction is the *pueblos blancos (see p105)*, in particular Grazalema, Zahara and Arcos de la Frontera, and the Roman ruins at Ronda la Vieja.

**Puente Nuevo, Ronda**

## 9 Drive from Guadalquivir Valley, Córdoba Province

**MAP D3**

Starting to the east of Córdoba, in the attractive hill town of Montoro, follow the river downstream. West of Córdoba, visit the once-fabulous Medina Azahara *(see p125)*, enjoy the view from Almodóvar del Río's castle walls and end at Palma del Río.

## 10 Drive in Las Alpujarras, Sierra Nevada

**MAP F4**

A region of villages and hamlets, many perched on the slopes of the Sierra Nevada. Begin at Lanjarón, then head for Órgiva market town. Continuing eastward, the landscape becomes more arid; eventually you will come to Yegen, made famous by Gerald Brenan's *South from Granada*.

---

**TOP 10 TOWN AND CITY WALKS**

**Córdoba's Jewish quarter**

**1 Seville**
Once you've done the main city-centre sights, head across the Puente de Isabel II and into the old gypsy quarter of Triana *(see p88)*.

**2 Granada**
Lose yourself in  maze of hilly streets in the Albaicín district *(see pp16–17)*.

**3 Córdoba**
Have a free-form wander around the ancient Jewish quarter and then make for the Puente Romano for sunset views *(see pp22–5)*.

**4 Cádiz**
Start at the northeast corner of Plaza de España and circumambulate the city, taking in the seascapes and gardens *(see pp26–7)*.

**5 Jerez**
Stroll through the Barrio de Santiago, the town's gypsy quarter *(see p106)*.

**6 Ronda**
Cross the Puente Nuevo, turn left and follow the town clockwise, being sure to pass the main church *(see pp30–31)*.

**7 Baeza**
From charming Plaza del Pópulo most of the main sights are found within walking distance, in a counter-clockwise direction *(see pp34–5)*.

**8 Úbeda**
Take a westerly walk to the monumental Hospital de Santiago and the Plaza de Toros *(see pp34–5)*.

**9 Málaga**
Tour Málaga's historic sights north of the Paseo del Parque *(see p104)*.

**10 Antequera**
This ancient town's main attractions are at the foot of the Alcazaba, but enjoy the views from above *(see p104)*.

# Children's Attractions

### 1 Muelle de las Carabelas, La Rábida, Huelva

MAP A4 ▪ Paraje de La Rábida
▪ 959 53 05 97 ▪ Open mid-Jun–mid-Sep: 10:30am–9:30pm Tue–Sun; mid-Sep–mid-Jun: 9:30am–8pm Tue–Sun ▪ Closed 1 Jan, 24, 25 & 31 Dec ▪ Adm; under 5s and disabled free

Down by the waterfront, the "Pier of the Caravels" is a great treat for kids. They'll love the chance to climb aboard full-size replicas of Columbus's ships *Niña*, *Pinta* and *Santa María* and imagine themselves setting sail to discover the New World. There's also a small museum and a recreation of a 15th-century European village (see p97).

**Replica ships, Muelle de las Carabelas**

### 2 Parque Zoológico, Jerez

Primarily, this is a care station for the rehabilitation of injured animals, in particular indigenous endangered species. Children can have a close-up encounter with the wonderful Iberian lynx, which is very rare in the wild. There are also white tigers and red pandas (see p58).

### 3 Isla Mágica, Seville

MAP K1 ▪ Pabellón España, Isla de Cartuja ▪ 902 16 17 16 ▪ Hours vary, call ahead for opening times ▪ Adm ▪ www.islamagica.es

This amusement park, occupying part of what was Expo '92, recreates the exploits of the 16th-century explorers who set out on voyages of discovery – rides have names such as Jaguar and Anaconda. There are also boat tours and a range of shows.

### 4 Carromato de Max, Mijas

MAP D5 ▪ Avda del Compás ▪ 952 58 90 34 ▪ Open Easter–Oct: 10am–8pm daily (to 10pm Jul & Aug); Nov–Easter: 10am–6pm daily ▪ Adm

This oddball collection claims to be a compendium of the world's smallest curiosities. There's a fine copy of Da Vinci's *The Last Supper* executed on a grain of rice, fleas in suits and Churchill's head sculpted in chalk.

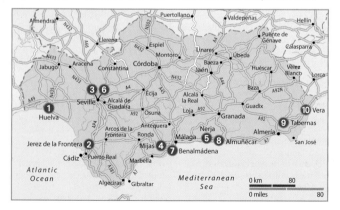

**Impressive mineral formations in the Cuevas de Nerja**

### ⑤ Cuevas de Nerja
MAP E5 ■ Ctra Maro ■ 952 52 95 20 ■ Open Easter & Jul–Aug: 9am–5:30pm Thu–Sat; Sep–Jun: 9am–3pm daily ■ Closed 1 Jan & 15 May ■ Adm ■ www.cuevadenerja.es

Only discovered in 1959, these caves go back some five million years. The chambers will stimulate a child's imagination – with a little help from fanciful names and evocative lighting. The central column in Cataclysm Hall is the tallest in the world.

### ⑥ Acuario Sevilla
MAP M6 ■ Muelle de las Delicias, Área Sur, Seville Port ■ 955 44 15 41 ■ Opening times vary, see website for details ■ Adm ■ www. acuariosevilla.es

Themed around Portuguese explorer Ferdinand Magellan's 1519–22 circum-navigation of the globe, the aquarium takes visitors on a tour of the under-water world. It houses some 7,000 sea creatures and reptiles, but the main attraction is a 9-metre (30-ft) deep tank of bull sharks.

### ⑦ Tívoli World, Benalmádena
MAP D5 ■ Avda de Tívoli ■ 952 57 70 16 ■ Opening times vary monthly, see website for more details ■ Adm ■ www.tivoli.es

Attractions at this theme park include a flamenco extravaganza and a Wild West show. With over 40 rides, Tívoli World is a great place for kids to have fun.

### ⑧ Aqua Tropic, Almuñécar
MAP F5 ■ Playa de Velilla, Paseo Reina Sofia ■ 958 63 20 81 ■ Open mid-Jun–Sep: 11am–7pm daily ■ Adm ■ www.aqua-tropic.com

Hours of fun, with rides called Kamikazee, Wavebreaker, Ring Rapids, Blackhole Rapids, Soft Runs and a Children's Lake for little ones.

### ⑨ Mini Hollywood, Almería
The Wild West rides again at this old "spaghetti western" movie set. At show time, kids can see Jesse James in action (see p118).

**The streets of Mini Hollywood**

### ⑩ Parque Acuático Vera
MAP H4 ■ Ctra Vera/Garrucha-Villaricos ■ 950 46 73 37 ■ Open mid-May–Jun & Sep: 11am–6pm daily; Jul & Aug: 11am–7:30pm daily ■ Adm ■ www.aquavera.com

This place will save the day when what your children need most is to cool off. There are five pools of various sizes, loads of undulating slides and tubes, as well as shaded areas.

# 🔟 Andalucian Dishes

### 1 Gazpacho

This signature Andalucian dish is a cold soup made of fresh tomatoes, green peppers, cucumber, garlic, olive oil, wine vinegar or lemon, breadcrumbs and salt. There are dozens of local variations of this nourishing refresher, which may involve almonds, grapes, melon, strawberries, red peppers and boiled egg or chopped ham garnishes. Perfect for a light lunch.

**Battered *calamares* and prawns**

*Tortilla española*

### 2 Tortilla Española and Patatas Bravas

Both of these dishes are ubiquitous not just in Andalucía but all over Spain. The first is a dense potato omelette with onions, fried into a savoury cake. It is served cold, by the slice, and is so filling it can make a full meal. The second consists of fried potato wedges served with a spicy tomato sauce and mayonnaise.

### 3 Fish Soups

The array of *sopas de mariscos* or *pescado* (shellfish or fish soups) seems to be limited only to the cook's imagination. Málaga favourites include *sopa viña*, a sherry-spiked version, and *cachoreñas*, with orange flavouring. Cádiz is known for its *guisos marineros* (seafood stews), made with the best seasonal fish of the region.

### 4 Calamares

All along the coast, you will encounter whole baby *calamares* (squids) served grilled – the essence of simplicity and delicious as long as they are fresh. A common alternative is to cut them into rings and batter-fry them – again, if they are fresh, they will taste sweet and tender. A complete *fritura de pescado* or *fritura mixta* (mixed fried fish) might add anchovies, prawns, chunks of cod or whatever is fresh that day.

### 5 Arroz a la Marinera

This is the Andalucian version of *paella*, an appellation that also appears on some menus. Saffron-flavoured rice is served with an assortment of fish and shellfish,

*Arroz a la marinera*

which can include prawns, clams and squid. Unlike the Valencia variety, it does not generally include sausage or chicken. The dish is also known as *arroz con mariscos*.

**6 Monkfish**
Monkfish *(rape)*, also called anglerfish, is one of the top choices for maritime eating in Andalucía. Only the tail of this unprepossessing looking fish is eaten, and it has a succulent quality similar to lobster tail or scallops. It is preferably served grilled, but can also be stewed in a rich sauce, usually tomato-based.

**7 Tocino de Cielo**
This rich egg custard pudding was traditionally made by nuns in Jerez de la Frontera.

*Tocino de cielo*, "heavenly custard"

**8 Salads**
Andalucian *ensaladas* (salads) are substantial and often include asparagus, boiled eggs, artichoke, carrots, olives, tuna and onions, in addition to lettuce and tomato.

**9 Valle de los Pedroches**
This soft sheep's cheese from Córdoba Province is typical of the regional type: strong in taste. The cheese is preserved in olive oil and enhanced with herbs.

**10 Dessert Tarts**
Cakes and sweet biscuits here typically involve Moorish ingredients such as anise, sesame, almonds and cinnamon. Most are sweetened with honey rather than sugar. Two common types are *alfajores*, with honey and almonds, and *piononos*, sometimes soaked in liqueur.

**TOP 10 DRINKS**

**1 Sherry**
The region's most famous wine comes from Cádiz Province *(see pp76–7)*.

**2 Brandy**
Brandy is distilled in Cádiz Province, Córdoba Province and Huelva Province.

**3 Wine**
Málaga's sweet wines come from Moscatel and Pedro Ximénez grapes, while fruity Condado wines are produced from Zalema grapes.

**4 Beer**
Cruzcampo is a local, Pilsner-type *cerveza* (beer) that is popular throughout the whole of Spain.

**5 Liqueur**
Aniseed-based liqueurs come primarily from Montilla in Córdoba Province. Other liqueurs include *aguardiente* from Huelva Province and *cazalla* from Sevilla Province.

**6 Sangría**
This classic red wine punch is world famous. The lighter *Tinto de Verano* is very popular in Andalucía.

**7 Coffee**
Opt for *café solo* (espresso) or *cortado* (espresso with very little milk). *Café con leche* (coffee with milk) is drunk by Spaniards for breakfast.

**8 Mint Tea**
Granada is particularly famous for its Moroccan-style tearooms, and *teterías* serving mint tea are popping up more and more *(see p122)*.

**9 Soft Drinks**
*Refrescos* include *batidos* (milkshakes), *granizados* (iced fruit crush) and *horchata* (a milky drink made from the tuber of the tigernut plant, or *chufa*).

**10 Mineral Water**
Choose *sin gas* (still) or *con gas* (fizzy), the best being from Lanjarón, Granada.

**Sherry from the barrel**

#  Tapas Dishes

### 1 Ensaladilla

"Russian salad" is sometimes an option for vegetarians – but not for vegans, as it usually consists of diced vegetables mixed in a thick mayonnaise. Watch out, however, as there are versions with cubes of ham mixed in as well. And make sure that this, and all mayonnaise-based dishes, are freshly prepared.

### 2 Chorizo al Vino

*Chorizos* are spicy, paprika- and garlic-flavoured red sausages that can be served grilled, sautéed with wine (*al vino*), or stewed with other ingredients. They are generally made of pork. *Morcilla* (blood sausage or black pudding) is a classic country delicacy.

*Chorizo al vino*

### 3 Mariscos

*Berberechos* (cockles), *almejas* (clams), *mejillones* (mussels), *pulpo* (octopus), *sepia* (cuttlefish) and *zamburiñas* (baby clams) are favourite seafood options everywhere in Spain. Roasted *caracoles* (snails), prepared with garlic, can be a rich but delicious treat.

### 4 Aceitunas

There are innumerable types of olives, from small to large, green to black, salty to sweet or whole to stuffed. The name of the dish can be confusing – although the Spanish

*Aceitunas* from Andalucía

name for the tree is the *olivo*, which comes from Latin, the word for the fruit comes from the Arabic *az-zait*, which means "juice of the olive".

### 5 Champiñones al Ajillo

Mushrooms sautéed with garlic are a regular on tapas menus. Other popular vegetable dishes include *judías* (green beans), often stewed with tomatoes and garlic, and *escalibadas* (roasted peppers) or *pisto*, the Spanish version of ratatouille.

### 6 Jamón Serrano

A complimentary slice of ham laid over the top of a *copa* (glass) is said to be how the custom of tapas (which literally means "lid") got started. The finest regional type available is mountain-cured ham, but there is also *jamón york* (regular ham), as well as other cured pork products, including a local *tocino* (bacon) and *fiambres* (cold cuts). It's particularly fine when eaten with local cheese and bread.

*Tabla serrana*

### 7 Albóndigas
"Meatballs" can be made from meat or fish and will most likely be stewed in a tomato sauce, together with garlic and spices. An alternative method of preparing chunks of meat, seafood or fish is by skewering them and grilling them as kebabs, either plain or spicy Moroccan-style.

### 8 Anchoas (Boquerones)
Anchovies and sardines are commonly served lightly fried in batter, but can just as likely be offered marinated and preserved in oil, or with a tomato sauce. You generally eat them minus the head but with all the bones.

*Anchoas*

### 9 Croquetas
Chicken or fish and mashed potatoes are mixed with béchamel and deep-fried to create these popular croquettes. A variation on this theme are *soldaditos* (fritters), which can be made of vegetables, chicken or fish.

*Croquetas*

### 10 Alioli
This is mayonnaise laced with garlic and is served as a dish in its own right, for dipping bread into or as a condiment. Another popular relish is *pipirrana*, a compote made of tomato, onion and pepper.

**TOP 10 TAPAS PREPARATION STYLES**

A selection of tapas and bread

**1 Pickled**
Mixed in with olives, you'll often find miniature gherkins, and possibly pearl onions, bits of garlic and hot peppers.

**2 Marinated**
Anchovies, sardines and seafood all come marinated. You'll see them sitting out on bars, possibly under glass, steeped in olive oil.

**3 Cured**
The hams of Andalucía are lightly salted – mountain-cured are the best.

**4 With Mayonnaise**
Any dish can be an excuse to slather on the *alioli*. Two dishes that often have mayonnaise are *patatas alioli* and *ensaladilla*.

**5 On Bread**
Many tapas don't really come to life until applied to bread. Some are served already perched on a slice.

**6 Egg-Based**
Eggs are essential in *tortilla (see p72)* or come hard-boiled as a garnish.

**7 Fried**
Almost anything you can think of will turn up *frito* (batter-fried or sautéed), from fish to mushrooms.

**8 Grilled or Roasted**
If you want to ingest a little less oil, *a la plancha* (grilled) and *asado* (roasted) are the options to choose.

**9 Stewed**
*Estofado* variations include fish, meat, potato and vegetables, often cooked in tomato sauce.

**10 A la Marinera**
This technique, commonly used for fish and seafood, is similar to poaching and involves wine, garlic and parsley.

# ⬛🔟 Bodegas and Wineries

**Barrels of sherry fill the impressive Moorish cellars at Pedro Domecq**

### ① Pedro Domecq
MAP B5 ▪ C/San Ildefonso 3, Jerez de la Frontera ▪ 956 15 15 00 ▪ Tours at noon, 2pm & 4pm Mon–Fri, noon Sat (hourly visits to different parts of the bodega) ▪ Adm ▪ www.bodegasfundadorpedrodomecq.com

One of the most legendary of the names associated with sherry. The company was founded in 1730, and a tour of the famous Moorish-style cellar "de la Ina" is *de rigueur* when in Jerez (see p106).

**Family-run González-Byass**

### ② González-Byass
MAP B5 ▪ C/Manuel María González 12, Jerez ▪ 956 35 70 16 ▪ Tour timings vary, check website for details ▪ Adm ▪ www.bodegastiopepe.com

Although most of the main sherry producers are now largely owned by British multinationals, encouragingly, this *bodega* was bought back by the family. Founded in 1835, their operation has two historic cellars, as well as the original tasting room.

### ③ Osborne Bodega
MAP B5 ▪ C/Los Moros, El Puerto de Santa María, Cadiz ▪ 956 86 91 00 ▪ Tours by appt ▪ Adm ▪ www.osborne.es

The black bull seen on Andalucian roadside hills is the symbol of this venerable sherry and brandy maker and a part of regional heritage.

### ④ Sandeman
MAP B5 ▪ C/Pizarro 10, Jerez ▪ 675 64 71 77 ▪ Regular, timed tours and tastings, see website for details ▪ Adm ▪ www.sandeman.com

The distinctive silhouetted figure of The Don, in a black cape and wide-brimmed hat, dates from 1928 and is one of the first trademark images ever created. Sandeman was founded in London in 1790.

### ⑤ Bodegas Robles, Montilla
MAP D3 ▪ Ctra. Córdoba-Málaga km 47 ▪ 957 65 00 63 ▪ Tours by appt ▪ www.bodegasrobles.com

This organic wine producer employs an old system called *solera*, in which young wines are blended with older ones, until they mature.

### ⑥ Bodegas Alvear, Montilla
What distinguishes the wines here is two-fold. Giant terracotta containers *(tinajas)* are sunk into the ground to keep the contents at a constant temperature, while the hot climate ripens the grapes for a stronger wine (see p126).

### 7 Bodegas Gomara

MAP E5 ▪ Pol. Campanilla 232, Diseminado Maqueda Alto 59, Málaga ▪ 952 43 41 95 ▪ Tours by appt ▪ www.gomara.com

This *bodega* produces the traditional Málaga wines and its own *fino*. It sells souvenir bottles shaped and painted like matadors, guitars or castanets.

### 8 Bodegas Antonio Barbadillo

MAP B5 ▪ C/Luís de Eguilaz 11, Sanlúcar de Barrameda ▪ 956 38 55 00 ▪ English tours 11am Tue–Sat or by appt ▪ Adm ▪ www.barbadillo.com

A family-owned winery with 5 sq km (2 sq miles) of vineyards, the largest cellars in Sanlúcar and a museum on wine making. Barbadillo launched its first *manzanilla* in 1827 and now produces a range of wines, including one of Spain's best whites.

**Bodegas Antonio Barbadillo**

### 9 Bodegas Andrade

MAP A4 ▪ Av de la Coronación 35, Bollullos Par del Condado, Huelva ▪ 959 41 01 06 ▪ Tours by appt ▪ www.bodegasandrade.es

This *bodega* was one of the first to realize the potential of the Zalema grape for creating young wines.

### 10 Agroalimentaria Virgen del Rocío

MAP B4 ▪ Av Cabezudos 3, Almonte, Huelva ▪ 959 40 61 46 ▪ Tours by appt ▪ www.raigal.es

A series of fermenting vats form a subterranean cellar, where the Zalema grape is used to produce one of the region's few sparkling wines, Raigal.

## TOP 10 SHERRIES AND WINES

**Andalucian sherry**

**1 Fino**
Clear, crisp and dry, with an aroma of almonds, *fino* sherry is served chilled as an aperitif.

**2 Manzanilla**
The *fino* sherry made in Sanlúcar de Barrameda, Cádiz Province. It is dry, pale and slightly salty.

**3 Oloroso**
The layer of flor yeast is thin, or absent, as a *fino* ages, allowing partial oxidation. *Oloroso* is a rich amber, with an aroma of hazelnuts.

**4 Amontillado**
Midway between a *fino* and an *oloroso*. The layer of flor yeast is allowed to die off, so it gets darker in colour.

**5 Palo Cortado**
This has an aroma reminiscent of an *amontillado*, while its colour is closer to *oloroso*.

**6 Cream Sherry**
This international favourite results when you take an *oloroso* and sweeten it by mixing in a measure of Pedro Ximénez wine.

**7 Pedro Ximénez**
This naturally sweet wine, when aged with care, is elegant and velvety.

**8 Brandy de Jerez**
Produced only in Jerez, it is sweeter and more caramelized than French brandy. It is made by ageing wine spirits in casks that have previously been used to age sherry.

**9 Málaga**
Málaga's famous sweet wines are made from the Moscatel and Pedro Ximénez grape varieties.

**10 Raigal**
One of Andalucía's few sparkling wines, this is refreshing on the palate.

# ⊞⊞ Andalucía for Free

### ① Archivo General de Indias, Seville

The UNESCO-listed archives building was commissioned by Philip II in 1573 as a merchant's exchange and designed by architect Juan de Herrera (who worked on El Escorial). It contains more than 80 million documents, including letters sent by Columbus to his royal patrons, Ferdinand and Isabella *(see p54)*.

### ② Cathedral, Seville

Normally you pay to wander around the magnificent 15th-century cathedral, set on the rectangular base of an Almohad mosque, but services here are free. There are choral masses at 8:30am daily from October to May *(see pp18–9)*.

### ③ Torre del Oro, Seville

This 12-sided military watchtower built by the Almohad dynasty in the 13th century was used to control access to Seville via the Guadalquivir river and later became a prison. Its golden sheen comes from its building materials – mortar, lime and pressed hay – reflected in the river. Visitors can enter for free on Mondays *(see p85)*.

### ④ Patios, Córdoba

Since Roman and Moorish times, Córdoba citizens have used their inner courtyards to

**Pretty patio in Córdoba**

gossip and drink tea or take in the air on sultry summer days and nights. Many of the oldest are in the Alcázar Viejo district, between the Alcázar and San Basilio. There are more in Santa Marina, around the church of San Lorenzo and near la Magdalena, and in Judería. Guides take groups on tours but you may explore those open to the public for yourself. At the beginning of May, for 12 days, Córdoba celebrates the Fiesta of the Patios – an event included on UNESCO's Intangible Heritage list since 2012.

### ⑤ Mirador de San Nicolas, Granada

Go up to this high plaza to see a panoramic view of the Alhambra and surrounding districts and, on clear days, the peaks of the Sierra Nevada. It's just a short walk up the hill from Plaza Nueva through the winding cobblestone alleys of the Albaicín area. There are hop-on, hop-off buses for those with limited mobility.

**Torre del Oro, Seville**

### 6 Street Art, Granada

Far removed from the ancient artistic wonders of the Alhambra, Granada's side streets and walls provide rough canvases for designs by talented street artists. Some are inspired by abstract expressionist painter José Guerrero, and much of the work is witty as well as gritty.

### 7 Centro de Arte Contemporáneo, Málaga

MAP E5 ▪ C/Alemania
▪ 952 12 00 55 ▪ www.cacmalaga.eu
The CAC has a permanent display of international artists including pieces by Louise Bourgeois, Olafur Eliasson, Thomas Hirschhorn and Damian Hirst, as well as post-1980s Spanish art, plus rotating temporary shows.

### 8 Fundación Picasso Casa Natal, Málaga

MAP E5 ▪ Plaza de la Merced 15
▪ 951 92 60 60 ▪ www.fundacion picasso.malaga.eu
The birthplace museum of Picasso, housing an array of his art, is free on Sundays between 4pm and 8pm.

**Roman theatre, Ruinas de Acinipo**

### 9 Ruinas de Acinipo, near Ronda

MAP D5 ▪ Ctra Ronda-Sevilla km22
▪ 952 18 71 19
Founded in 45 BC to house retired soldiers from the Roman legions, the Acinipo ruins include a Roman theatre that is still in use today.

### 10 El Torcal de Antequera

Known for its striking limestone rock formations, El Torcal offers excellent hiking terrain. There are three marked routes taking from 30 minutes to three hours (see p60).

**TOP 10 MONEY-SAVING TIPS**

**Tapas, free with a drink**

**1** Access free Wi-Fi at bars and cafés in most towns and in hotel lobbies.

**2** In Granada – city and province – tapas still come free with every drink. The custom extends to some bars in Almería and Jaén province.

**3** Buy a tourist pass (bono turístico). The Granada Card, Málaga Card and Sevilla Card cover public transport and offer discounts or free entry to sights. Prices vary. Jaén, Úbeda, Baeza and Ronda also have discount bonos.

**4** Avoid Marbella, especially Puerto Banús; prices reflect the VIP visitors.

**5** If you are a visitor from outside the EU and are leaving with purchased goods to the value of €90.15 or more, get a refund on Spain's 21 per cent sales tax (VAT, known here as IVA).

**6** "Exotic" cuisines from, say, India or Thailand, are pricey. Regional cuisine tends to be the best value.

**7** Avoid the tourist-heavy flamenco shows in Seville and aim instead for bars and clubs in Triana and elsewhere where local singers perform for local people. Ask for recommendations at the tourist office or your hotel.

**8** Don't go near any of the major cities around Easter Week (Semana Santa). Room rates can go through the roof, especially at the smarter hotels. August can also be an expensive month.

**9** Consider camping, especially if walking in Grazalema, the Alpujarra or Sierra Nevada. The sites tend to be at a high altitude and so relatively cool and pleasant, even in summer. Prices start at €5 per night per tent.

**10** At lunch, ask for the "menú del día" – or daily special. It is often as little as €7 and may be a tasty stew or fish dish.

# Religious Festivals

### ① Fiesta de los Reyes Magos
**5 Jan**

Traditionally, this evening commemorates the arrival of the Three Kings at the infant Jesus's manger crib. Parades across the region feature the trio, lavishly dressed, progressing through towns in small carriages drawn by tractors or horses. The next day, Epiphany, is the day that children receive gifts.

**Revellers celebrating at Carnaval**

### ② Carnaval
**Feb**

Most Andalucian towns celebrate this Catholic festival, the most spectacular extravaganza being in Cádiz. Costumes and masked balls are the order of the day and night during these chaotic revels. The implicit anarchy invites every sort of political lampoon, which is why Franco tried to abolish these events (see p27).

### ③ Semana Santa
**Easter week**

Holy Week is observed in every town and village in the region, with dramatic and spectacular processions, especially in Seville. Effigies of Christ and the Virgin are carried through the streets on huge floats. Dressed in traditional outfits, people either maintain penitential silence or express commiseration with the suffering Lord and His mournful Mother (see p19).

### ④ Romerías
**May–Oct**

Taking part in one of these local festivals is an experience no visitor will forget – almost every community has its own romería. Usually, the programme involves a colourful pilgrimage to a shrine outside of town, followed by days of merry-making. The name may recall ancient pilgrimages, when devotees walked to Rome (see p36).

### ⑤ Corpus Christi
**Dates vary**

This festival celebrates the miracle of Transubstantiation, when the Host becomes the body of Christ and the wine, His blood. Granada's celebration is the most famous, with parades and partying, followed by bullfights and flamenco.

**Corpus Christi procession**

###  Fiesta de las Cruces
3 May

The Festival of the Crosses celebrates the discovery of the True Cross by St Helena in the 4th century. Modes of veneration vary widely in the region, but may include competitions for producing the most gorgeous flower-decked cross.

### 7 San Juan
23 & 24 Jun

This feast, in celebration of John the Baptist, is important in many parts of Andalucía. Midsummer fireworks and bonfires seem to be the order of the day in most communities.

### 8 Virgen del Carmen
15 & 16 Jul

The patron saint of sailors is all-important in coastal communities. Statues of the Virgin are put onboard a flower-adorned fishing boat and floated out to sea and back again, amid music, fireworks and cheering.

**Virgen del Carmen festival**

### 9 Ascension of the Virgin
15 Aug

At the height of the summer heat, the Virgin Mary's ascension into heaven is celebrated. There is much socializing, drinking and dancing. The day marks the beginning of the Feria de Málaga, a week-long party.

### 10 Fiesta de San Miguel
Last week Sep–first week Oct

This mix of bullfights, exhibitions and dancing is particularly noteworthy in Seville, Úbeda and the Albaicín quarter of Granada. In Torremolinos, it closes the summer season in festive style. .

## TOP 10 FERIAS AND OTHER FESTIVALS

**Riders at Feria del Caballo**

**1 Flamenco Festivals**
These take place during the summer months all around the region.

**2 Moros y Cristianos**
Festivals centre on re-enactments of Christian take-overs of various towns and take place throughout the year.

**3 Feria de Abril**
Held in Seville two weeks after Easter, this is the largest fair in Spain *(see p86)*.

**4 Feria del Caballo**
May
This fair in Jerez de la Frontera centres on Andalucian horses.

**5 Music and Dance Festivals**
The most famous of these takes place in Granada from late June to early July.

**6 Wine Festivals**
Celebrations of the fruit of the vine occur from April to September, when *La Vendimia* (grape harvest) happens.

**7 Sherry Festivals**
Sep–Oct
The towns of the "Sherry Triangle" *(see p106)* celebrate their fortified wines at various times, notably in Jerez.

**8 Feria de Jamón**
15 Aug
Late summer and autumn sees the traditional *matanza* (slaughter) of pigs and several celebrations of ham, notably in Trevélez.

**9 Fiesta de la Aceituna**
1st week Dec
The olive is celebrated in the Jaén Province town of Martos.

**10 Fiesta de los Verdiales**
28 Dec
In Málaga Province at Puerta de la Torre, this is a day for practical jokes and a chance to wear funny hats. It dates back to Moorish times.

# Top 10 Andalucía and the Costa del Sol Area by Area

The Roman Bridge crossing the Río Guadalquivir in Córdoba

# 🔟 Seville

Andalucía's capital is an aristocratic yet relaxed city, with a fabulous cultural heritage that dates back beyond recorded history.

**Mudéjar-style tiles at Casa de Pilatos**

Its fate has always been tied to the Río Guadalquivir ("the great river" in Arabic), and the trade it offered the city. Today, much of the riverfront is made up of an attractive promenade. There is a wealth of art and architecture to see in the historic centre of Seville as well as distinctive neighbourhoods, each with their own charm. But its highlights, including the splendid cathedral, Moorish and Renaissance palaces and fine museums, are within walking distance of each other.

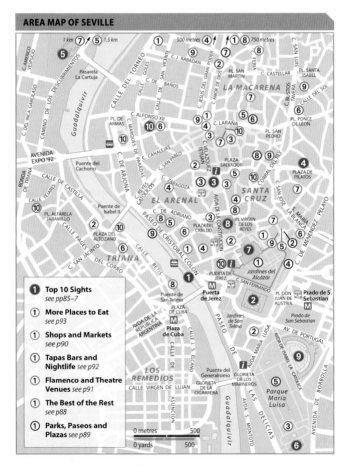

**AREA MAP OF SEVILLE**

1. Top 10 Sights
   see pp85–7
1. More Places to Eat
   see p93
1. Shops and Markets
   see p90
1. Tapas Bars and
   Nightlife see p92
1. Flamenco and Theatre
   Venues see p91
1. The Best of the Rest
   see p88
1. Parks, Paseos and
   Plazas see p89

**River view of the Torre del Oro**

### 1 Torre del Oro and Torre de la Plata

MAP L4 ■ Torre del Oro: Paseo de Colón ■ 954 22 24 19 ■ Open 9:30am–6:45pm Mon–Fri, 10:30am–6:45pm Sat–Sun; Adm (except Mon) ■ Torre de Plata: C/Santander 15 ■ No public entry

Tradition states that the imposing 13th-century Moorish dodecahedral (12-sided) watchtower, the Torre del Oro (Tower of Gold), is named after the golden tiles that once adorned it. Others say its name derives from its use as a warehouse for the gold coming in from the New World during Seville's heyday. It now houses a small maritime museum. Nearby stands the Torre de Plata (Tower of Silver), a more modest octagonal tower, which most likely gets its name as a complement to its neighbour. Both towers originally formed part of the city's defences.

### 2 Real Fábrica de Tabacos

MAP M5 ■ C/San Fernando 4 ■ Open 8am–8:30pm Mon–Fri

Now a part of Seville University, this handsome 18th-century edifice is the second-largest building in Spain, after El Escorial in Madrid. Famous for its fun-loving female workers, who at one time rolled three-quarters of Europe's cigars, the old factory has been immortalized by *Carmen*, the world's most popular opera. The doomed heroine, a hot-blooded gypsy *cigarrera*, remains, for many, a symbol of Spanish passion.

### 3 Ayuntamiento

MAP L3 ■ Plaza Nueva 1 ■ 955 47 02 64 ■ Open for pre-booked guided tours (only online), mid-Sep–May: 5:30 & 6pm Tue–Thu (6pm & 6:30pm Jun), 10am Sat

This building has been the town hall since the 16th century. Inside, the rooms are decorated with historic paraphernalia of the city and the monarchy, in a blend of Gothic and Renaissance styles. Outside, the façades reflect the evolution of taste, from the original Renaissance Plateresque work with its finely carved stonework, to the 19th-century attempt to copy the style, seen from Plaza de San Francisco.

### 4 Casa de Pilatos

MAP N3 ■ Plaza de Pilatos 1 ■ 954 22 52 98 ■ Open 9am–6pm daily (to 7pm Apr–Oct) ■ Adm (free Tue for EU members)

Erroneously said to be based on the house of Pontius Pilate in Jerusalem, this 15th-century gem is the most sumptuous of Seville's urban mansions. It is a delightful blend of Mudéjar, Gothic and Renaissance styles, punctuated with Classical statuary. Look for the carved head of the Greek boy, Antinous, who drowned and was deified by his grief-stricken lover, Emperor Hadrian, in the 2nd century *(see p50)*.

**Courtyard passage, Casa de Pilatos**

### 5 Monasterio de la Cartuja de Santa María de las Cuevas

MAP J1 ■ Centro Andaluz de Arte Contemporáneo ■ 955 03 70 70 ■ Open 11am–9pm Tue–Sat, 10am–3:30pm Sun; Adm (free 7–9pm Tue–Fri and all day Sat) ■ www.caac.es

This 15th-century monastery has had its ups and downs over the centuries. During Spain's Golden Age, it was the favoured retreat of Christopher Columbus, whose remains were interred here for several decades. The monks went on to decorate their vast enclave with commissions from some of Seville's greatest artists – most of the works are now in the Museo de Bellas Artes (see p87). In 1841, it became a ceramics factory. Finally restored as part of Seville's Expo '92, the complex is today home to a contemporary art museum.

**Museo Arqueológico**

### 6 Museo Arqueológico

MAP N6 ■ Parque de María Luisa ■ 955 12 06 32 ■ Jun–mid-Sep: 9am–3:30pm Tue–Sat, 10am–5pm Sun; mid-Sep–May: 9am–8:30pm Tue–Sat, 9am–2:30pm Sun ■ Adm

This Renaissance-style pavilion was also one of the fabulous structures created for the 1929 Exposition and now houses Andalucía's principal archaeological museum. The assemblage of artifacts ranges from Paleolithic finds, exhibited in the basement, to splendours of Roman and Moorish art. The Carambolo treasures of Tartessian gold, also on display in the basement, and the Roman sculpture collection are outstanding.

**Water tanks under the Real Alcázar**

### 7 Real Alcázar

This exotic palace was primarily the brainchild of Pedro I, who had it built as a lavish love-nest for himself and his mistress, María de Padilla (see pp20–21).

### 8 Seville Cathedral and La Giralda

Legend has it that when the *sevillanos* decided to build their cathedral in the 15th century, they intended to erect an edifice so huge that later generations would call them mad. They achieved their aim with the largest church (by volume) in Christendom (see pp18–19).

**FERIA DE ABRIL**

The six-day Spring Fair (below), about two weeks after Easter, is a riot of colour and high spirits. Andalucian horses strut on parade, ridden by *caballeros* in traditional leather chaps, waistcoats and wide-brimmed *sombreros cordobeses*, often with dazzling women perched behind. The air is alive with music, the fairgrounds overflow with *casetas* (party marquees – most of them by invitation only), and partying continues until dawn. All festivities take place south of the river.

## 9 Plaza de España
MAP N6

This semicircular plaza was designed as the centrepiece for the Ibero-American Exposition of 1929. Almost completely covered with gorgeous glazed tiles, its surfaces depict historic moments and heraldic symbols of the 40 regions of Spain. A canal follows the arc of the structure, crossed by colourful footbridges. The site was used as a set in the film *Star Wars: Attack of the Clones*, for its other-worldly feel.

Gallery, Museo de Bellas Artes

## 10 Museo de Bellas Artes
MAP K2 ■ Plaza del Museo 9 ■ 955 54 29 42 ■ Open 16 Jun–15 Sep: 9am–3:30pm Tue–Sun; 16 Sep–15 Jun: 9am–8:30pm Tue–Sat, 9am–3:30pm Sun ■ Adm (free for EU members)

Second only to the Prado in Madrid for its range of great Spanish paintings. The collection is housed in a former 17th-century convent and focuses on the Seville School, led by Cano, Zurbarán, Valdés Leal and Murillo – look out for his touching *Virgen de la Servilleta*. Don't miss El Greco's poignant portrait of his son and the polychrome terracotta of St Jerome by Florentine sculptor Pietro Torregiano, a colleague of Michelangelo *(see p54)*.

### A WALK AROUND THE BARRIO DE SANTA CRUZ

#### ▶ MORNING

Start at the exit to the **Real Alcázar** *(see pp20–21)* on Patio de las Banderas. Turn right to find the **Arco de la Judería**, a covered alleyway that leads to the **Callejón del Agua**, running along the old Jewish Quarter's southern wall. Peep into some of the famously lush patios of these perfectly whitewashed houses. The writer Washington Irving once stayed at No. 2. After the wall ends, find the **Jardines de Murillo** on your right *(see p89)*, and enjoy a tranquil stroll.

Turn back to find **Plaza Santa Cruz** *(see p89)*, where the church that gave the neighbourhood its name once stood, until it was burned down by the French in 1810. A 17th-century wrought-iron cross stands here now. Cross a couple of streets west to find the **Hospital de los Venerables** *(see p88)*. Take in its delightful central courtyard and important art gallery.

For lunch, try traditional tapas at the old **Casa Plácido** *(see p93)*.

#### AFTERNOON

From here, go east to **Calle Santa Teresa 8**, the former home of the great artist Bartolomé Murillo *(see p48)*, who died here in 1682 after a fall while painting frescoes in Cádiz.

Finally, work your way back towards the **cathedral** *(see pp18–19)* along Calle Mesón del Moro and then to **Calle Mateos Gago**. At No 1 you'll find the **Cervecería Giralda** *(954 22 82 50)*, excellent for a drink or food at any time of day.

See map on p84 ←

# The Best of the Rest

**Valdés Leal frescoes, Hospital de los Venerables**

## 1 Hospital de los Venerables

MAP M4 ▪ Plaza de los Venerables 8 ▪ 954 56 26 96 ▪ Open 10am–6pm daily ▪ Adm

Founded in the 17th century as a home for the elderly, this is now a cultural centre. It features a *trompe-l'oeil* ceiling by Juan de Valdés Leal.

## 2 Archivo General de Indias

MAP M4 ▪ Avda de la Constitución 3 ▪ 954 50 05 28 ▪ Open 9:30am–5pm Mon–Sat, 10am–2pm Sun

This is a storehouse for documents on the Spanish colonization of the New World (see p54 & p78).

## 3 Museo de Artes y Costumbres Populares

MAP N6 ▪ Plaza de América 3 ▪ 955 54 29 51 ▪ Open 9am–8:30pm Tue–Sat (to 3:30pm Sun & summer) ▪ Adm

Exhibits here include displays on flamenco and bullfighting.

## 4 Hospital de la Caridad

MAP L4 ▪ C/Temprado 3 ▪ 954 22 32 32 ▪ Open 9am–1:30pm, 3:30–7:30pm Mon–Sat, 9am–1pm, 3:30–7:30pm Sun ▪ Adm

A hospital founded by reformed rake Miguel de Mañara, the inspiration for Don Juan. The chapel contains Baroque sculpture.

## 5 Real Maestranza

MAP L3 ▪ Paseo de Cristóbal Colón 12 ▪ 954 22 45 77 ▪ Open daily

The so-called "Cathedral of Bullfighting" becomes the focal point of Seville when the sporting season opens in April.

## 6 Barrio de Triana

MAP K4

This quarter, once home to Seville's gypsies, was known for producing bullfighters, flamenco artists and fine ceramics – which are still made today (see p90). Residents here are called *Trianeros*.

## 7 Casa de la Condesa de Lebrija

MAP M2 ▪ C/Cuna 8 ▪ 954 22 78 02 ▪ Open daily (Jul–Aug: Mon–Sat) ▪ Adm

A 15th-century, typically Sevillian mansion, embellished with mosaics from Itálica (see p97).

## 8 Cámara Oscura

MAP M1 ▪ C/Resolana ▪ 679 09 10 73 ▪ Open 11:30am–6pm Tue–Sun (weather permitting) ▪ Adm

Huge camera obscura displays a moving image of the area around the Torre de los Perdigones.

## 9 La Macarena

MAP N1

This district is home to the Rococo Iglesia de San Luis; the 15th-century Convento de Santa Paula; and Seville's adored religious icon, the Virgen de la Macarena. During Semana Santa (see p80) she is paraded on a float.

## 10 Museo del Baile Flamenco

MAP M3 ▪ C/Manuel Rojas Marcos 3 ▪ 954 34 03 11 ▪ Open 10am–7pm daily ▪ Adm

A museum exploring the wonderful world of flamenco dancing.

# Parks, Paseos and Plazas

### 1 Real Alcázar
These gardens are a blend of Moorish and Italian Renaissance styles *(see pp20–21)*.

### 2 Plaza Santa Cruz
MAP N4

Created when Napoleon's soldiers destroyed a church that stood here, this square is now adorned by an iron cross, La Cruz de la Cerrajería.

### 3 Plaza de San Francisco and Plaza Nueva
MAP L3 & M3

These squares represent the heart of the city. Plaza de San Francisco (also the Plaza Mayor, or main square) is Seville's oldest and hosts many public spectacles. Plaza Nueva is a pleasant park with a monument to King Fernando the Saint.

### 4 Jardines de Murillo
MAP N4

These formal gardens used to be the orchards and vegetable plots for the Alcázar. Donated to the city in 1911, they are named after Seville painter Bartolomé Murillo *(see p48)*. The Columbus monument features the bronze prows of the *Santa María*, the caravel that bore him to the New World in 1492.

### 5 Parque de María Luísa
MAP M6

This park dominates the southern end of the city. Its present design, comprising the immense Plaza de España, was laid out for the 1929 Exposition. Look for peacocks in the trees. Beware of pickpockets *(see p59)*.

**Parque de María Luísa**

### 6 Plaza de la Encarnación
MAP M2

This square is dominated by the intriguing architecture of the Metropol Parasol complex, with its shops, bars, observation deck, market and subterranean museum.

**Plaza de la Encarnación**

### 7 Alameda de Hércules
MAP M1

Set off by pairs of columns at either end – the southern set are ancient Roman – this popular promenade is lined with trendy bars and reateries, which draw a bohemian crowd.

### 8 Plaza de la Alfalfa
MAP M2

Once the location of the hay market, and later a Sunday morning pet market, the Alfalfa is now a good area for browsing. Visit clothing stores, flamenco boutiques, unique accessory shops and bars.

### 9 Paseo Alcalde Marqués de Contadero
MAP L4

With the Torre del Oro at one end *(see p85)*, this riverfront walkway makes for a pleasant stroll.

### 10 Calle San Fernando and Avenida de la Constitución
MAP M5

These two streets form a pedestrian promenade through the heart of Seville, livened up by art exhibitions.

*See map on p84*

# Shops and Markets

### 1 El Corte Inglés
MAP L2 ■ Plaza del Duque de la Victoria 8

Although you're unlikely to find any bargains here, the range of merchandise is impressive. Spain's main department store chain carries not only clothes and accessories, but also perfume, housewares and sporting goods. There's also a food hall and supermarket, which stock gourmet foods.

**Shop sign for Ceramica Triana**

### 2 Ceramica Triana
MAP J4 ■ C/Callao 14
■ 954 33 21 79

The place to buy the famous Triana pottery, this shop sells everything from replicas of 16th-century tiles to ashtrays. The old ceramics factory, a protected historical monument, is now a museum next door.

### 3 Mango
MAP L2 ■ C/O'Donnell 8

For the latest in younger women's fashion trends, at reasonable prices, this Spanish clothing brand is the place to go.

### 4 Zara
MAP L2 ■ C/del Duque de la Victoria (and other branches)

Spain's best-known high street fashion chain sells affordable clothing for the entire family.

### 5 Aurora Gaviño
MAP M3 ■ C/Álvarez Quintero 16 ■ 954 22 54 94

This is a good spot to load up on all the flouncy dresses, mantillas, shawls and so forth that you will need to participate in the various festivals that abound in the region (see pp80–81).

### 6 Art Market
MAP K2 ■ Plaza del Museo 9

On Sunday mornings from around 9am to 2pm, local artists display their works. Take home an original souvenir of Seville.

### 7 Botellas y Latas
MAP M1 ■ C/Regina 14
■ 954 29 31 22

This wine merchant and delicatessen has a large selection of gourmet regional produce and excellent Spanish wines. The owner, Carlos, is very welcoming.

### 8 El Mercadillo
MAP M1 ■ C/de la Feria
■ Every Thu 7am–3pm

Just off the Alameda de Hércules (see p89), El Jueves flea market is Seville's most famous second-hand market. It consists mostly of old junk, books and posters. Still, it's fun to look for the occasional treasure. But beware of pickpockets.

### 9 Hippy Market
MAP L2 ■ Plaza del Duque de la Victoria ■ Open Thu to Sat

This is the place to find hand-made jewellery, leather goods, unique clothes and other charming hand-crafted items.

### 10 Old Train Station Shopping Centre
MAP K2 ■ Antigua Estación de Córdoba, Plaza de Armas

Behind the exquisite Moorish façade, the old Córdoba train station is now home to a shopping, dining and entertainment complex.

# Flamenco and Theatre Venues

**Performance, Teatro de la Maestranza**

### 1 Teatro de la Maestranza
MAP L4 ■ Paseo de Cristobal Colón 22 ■ 954 22 33 44 ■ www.teatrodela maestranza.es

Built as part of Expo '92, Seville's main theatre serves primarily as the city's opera house, with productions of all the classics, particularly those set in Seville, including *Carmen, Don Juan, The Marriage of Figaro* and *The Barber of Seville*.

### 2 Teatro Lope de Vega
MAP M5 ■ Avda de María Luísa ■ 954 47 28 22 ■ Closed Jul–Aug ■ www.teatrolopedevega.org

This Neo-Baroque theatre, named after the "Spanish Shakespeare", was built in 1929 as a casino and theatre for the Ibero-American Exposition. Modern and classical works are performed here.

### 3 Teatro Quintero
MAP M2 ■ C/Cuna 15 ■ 954 50 02 92 ■ www.teatroquintero.com

This cultural hub is a theatre, stagecraft school and a TV studio.

### 4 Teatro Alameda
C/Crédito 11 ■ 954 90 01 64 ■ www.teatroalamedasevilla.org

Contemporary Andalucian drama and flamenco feature strongly at this popular, modest theatre.

### 5 Teatro Central
MAP J1 ■ C/José de Gálvez 6, Isla de Cartuja ■ 955 03 72 00 ■ Closed Jul–Sep

In season, this theatre highlights the *Flamenco Viene del Sur* series, alongside all sorts of theatre, dance and classical music. It's a starkly modern facility right on the river.

### 6 El Arenal
The least tacky of the flamenco shows aimed at tourists, although without the authenticity of the real thing. See the first show and the second is free. *(See p47.)*

### 7 La Carbonería
MAP N3 ■ C/Levies 18 ■ 954 56 37 49 ■ Shows Mon and Thu ■ www.levies18.com

A relaxed, authentic Flamenco bar with a good atmosphere.

### 8 El Patio Sevillano
MAP L4 ■ Paseo de Cristobal Colón 11A ■ 954 21 41 20 ■ Daily 7pm & 9:30pm ■ www.elpatiosevillano.com

Rousing flamenco shows to please the throngs of tourists.

**Flamenco dancers at El Patio Sevillano**

### 9 Los Gallos
MAP N4 ■ Plaza de Santa Cruz 11 ■ 954 21 69 81 ■ Daily 8pm & 10:30pm ■ www.tablaolosgallos.com

Despite its popularity with tourists, the atmosphere here is genuine. First-rate flamenco performers.

### 10 Casa de la Memoria de al-Andalus
MAP M2 ■ C/Cuna 6 ■ 954 56 06 70 ■ Daily 7:30pm and 9pm ■ www.casadelamemoria.es

Cultural centre dedicated to flamenco, hosting exhibitions, concerts and dance performances.

*See map on p84*

# Tapas Bars and Nightlife

**El Rinconcillo, arguably the most authentic tapas bar in Spain**

### 1 Sala Malandar Luxuria
MAP K1 ■ C/Torneo 43
■ 954 21 77 02 ■ No credit cards

Come to this laid back club for an eclectic array of music – from funk to reggae and ska via soul, folk and indie pop – by live bands and DJs.

### 2 Naima Café
MAP L1 ■ C/Trajano 47
■ 954 38 24 85 ■ No credit cards

Small but rich in atmosphere, this jazz bar has a relaxed feel. Jazz memorabilia adorns the wall, and there is live music at the weekend.

### 3 Casa Morales
MAP L3 ■ C/García de
Vinuesa 11 ■ 954 22 12 42

Reputedly the second-oldest bar in town (1850), and it doesn't seem to have changed much. Drinks are still poured from old casks. Simple tapas.

### 4 Antigüedades
MAP M3 ■ C/Argote de
Molina 40 ■ 954 56 51 27

The delightfully eccentric decor of this bar changes every few months, with masks, bizarre dolls or giant tarantulas. Reasonably priced beers attract locals and tourists alike.

### 5 GastroSol Tapas
MAP M2 ■ Plaza de la
Encarnación ■ 954 21 72 25

Six tapas bars share the same dining area in the *mirador* (viewing area) atop the Metropol Parasol complex. Outstanding views of the city centre.

### 6 El Rinconcillo
MAP M2 ■ C/Gerona 40
■ 954 22 31 83

The city's oldest *taberna* dates from 1670 and is an essential stop on your Seville itinerary. Said to be the place where tapas were invented.

### 7 Antique
C/Matemáticos Rey Pastor y
Castro, La Cartuja ■ 954 46 22 07

Dress to impress at Seville's most upscale club, and you might just get past the doormen. In summer, the terrace Aqua hosts live events.

### 8 La Terraza de EME
MAP M3 ■ C/Alemanes 27,
4th Floor of EME Catedral Hotel
■ 954 56 00 00

This is the place to see and be seen. Enjoy the spectacular views of the cathedral and the Giralda while sipping a cocktail on the terrace bar of the upmarket Eme hotel.

### 9 Bar El Garlochi
MAP M2 ■ C/Boteros 26
■ 663 62 39 04

A Seville institution with a unique religious decor. Expect Baroque exuberance and lively locals.

### 10 Puratasca
MAP J3 ■ C/Numancia 5
■ 954 33 16 21

Discover delicious twists on the classics at this friendly fusion tapas bar, where the menu changes with the seasons.

# More Places to Eat

 **1 Kiosco Restaurante Torre de Los Perdigones**
MAP L1 ▪ Calle Resolana 41
▪ 954 90 93 53 ▪ DA ▪ €

Located in a city park, this tapas bar and restaurant serves a modern take on classic Spanish dishes.

**2 El Aguador**
MAP L3 ▪ C/Albareda 14
▪ 954 22 47 20 ▪ €

This stylish restaurant offers regional cuisine with an imaginative twist. Try tender beef cheeks glazed with Pedro Ximénez sauce.

**3 Albarama**
MAP L3 ▪ Plaza de San Francisco 5 ▪ 954 22 97 84 ▪ €€

Facing Plaza de San Francisco, the modern decor here sets the mood for innovative dishes, such as *hamburguesa de atún con tartar de aguacate* (tuna burger with avocado tartare). Order tapas or plates.

**Taberna del Alabardero**

**4 Taberna del Alabardero**
MAP L3 ▪ C/Zaragoza 20
▪ 954 50 27 21 ▪ €€€

This superb restaurant has earned itself a Michelin star. The setting is sumptuous, while the menu excels in meat dishes and local seafood.

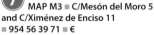

**PRICE CATEGORIES**
For a three-course meal for one with half a bottle of wine (or equivalent meal), taxes and extra charges
..................................................
€ under €30   €€ €30–€50   €€€ over €50

**5 La Albahaca**
MAP N4 ▪ Plaza Santa Cruz 12
▪ 954 22 07 14 ▪ €€

Set in a converted mansion, decorated with *azulejo* tiles. The seasonal menu may feature fish, wild mushroom dishes or game.

**6 Modesto**
MAP N4 ▪ C/Cano y Cueta 5
▪ 954 41 68 11 ▪ €

Enjoy garlic shrimp and excellent home-made paella at great value.

**7 Casa Plácido**
MAP M3 ▪ C/Mesón del Moro 5 and C/Ximénez de Enciso 11
▪ 954 56 39 71 ▪ €

Convenient for all the major sights, this venerable bar has hams dangling, barrels of sherry, old posters and traditional tapas.

**8 Abades Triana**
MAP L5 ▪ C/Betis 69
▪ 954 28 64 59 ▪ DA ▪ €€€

This modern restaurant has a commanding location on the river. Diners can book a spot in El Cubo, a private area with a "floating" glass floor. There are tapas, tasting and gourmet tasting menus on offer.

**9 Eslava**
MAP L1 ▪ C/Eslava 3–5
▪ 954 90 65 68 ▪ €

This excellent tapas bar offers specialities such as *costillas a la miel* (honeyed pork ribs).

**10 El Faro de Triana**
MAP K4 ▪ Puente de Isabel II
▪ 954 33 61 92 ▪ DA ▪ €€

On the Triana side of Seville's oldest bridge, this place has superb views, as well as simple, traditional food.

*See map on p84*

# TOP10 Sevilla and Huelva Provinces

Leaving behind the magnetic allure of glorious Seville, the rest of Sevilla Province and neighbouring Huelva Province are among the least visited areas of Andalucía. Consequently, much of the zone has remained a rural hinterland, where time moves slowly and the old customs prevail. Some of the finest nature preserves are here, too, including Parque Nacional de Doñana, mountainous reaches and pristine beaches, generally frequented by Spaniards rather than tourists. Culturally rich as well, each town and village shelters surprising art treasures and ancient marvels, where you may find yourself the only visitor – a welcome relief after the throngs encountered elsewhere in Andalucía.

**Bell tower, Écija**

## AREA MAP OF SEVILLA AND HUELVA PROVINCES

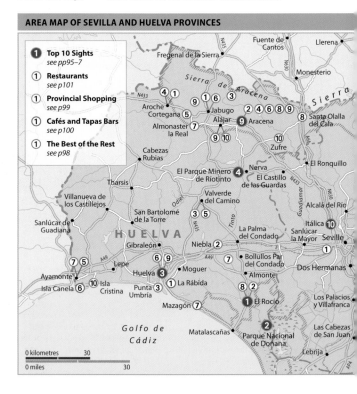

**1** Top 10 Sights
see pp95–7

**1** Restaurants
see p101

**1** Provincial Shopping
see p99

**1** Cafés and Tapas Bars
see p100

**1** The Best of the Rest
see p98

Fuente de Cantos

Llerena

Fregenal de la Sierra

Monesterio

Sierra de Aracena

Sierra

Aroche

Cortegana

Jabugo

Aracena

Santa Olalla del Cala

Almonaster la Real

Alàjar

Zufre

Cabezas Rubias

El Parque Minero de Riotinto

Nerva

El Castillo de las Guardas

El Ronquillo

Tharsis

Valverde del Camino

Villanueva de los Castillejos

San Bartolomé de la Torre

Alcalá del Río

Sanlúcar de Guadiana

Itálica

Gibraleón

Niebla

La Palma del Condado

Sanlúcar la Mayor

Seville

Ayamonte

Lepe

Huelva

Moguer

Bollullos Par del Condado

Almonte

Dos Hermanas

Isla Canela

Isla Cristina

Punta Umbría

La Rábida

El Rocío

Los Palacios y Villafranca

Mazagón

Las Cabezas de San Juan

Golfo de Cádiz

Matalascañas

Parque Nacional de Doñana

Lebrija

0 kilometres 30

0 miles 30

The Hermitage of El Rocío

### 1 El Rocío
MAP B4

The fact that this town resembles an Old West frontier outpost is no accident. The Spaniards who settled what are now the states of Texas, New Mexico and Arizona mostly came from this part of Spain and took their architectural style with them.

Horseback is still a normal way to get around. The place bursts into life during the annual Romería, one of Spain's biggest festivals (see p36).

### 2 Parque Nacional de Doñana

Europe's largest nature reserve has important wetlands and shifting dunes that are gradually moving inland. The fragile area can only be visited on guided tours (see pp36–7).

### 3 Huelva
MAP A4 ▪ Museo de Huelva: Alameda Sundheim 13 ▪ 959 65 04 24 ▪ Open mid-Jun–mid-Sep: 9am–3:30pm Tue–Sun; mid-Sep–mid-Jun: 9am–7:30pm Tue–Sat, 9am–3:30pm Sun ▪ Adm (free to EU members)

Founded by the Phoenicians, Huelva was at its peak under the Romans – Huelva's provincial museum holds remarkable archaeological finds. The city's other claim to fame is as the starting point of Columbus's epic voyage (see p43). Huelva was the first port for New World trade, before Seville took over.

El Parque Minero de Ríotinto

### 4 El Parque Minero de Ríotinto
MAP B3 ▪ Museo Minero: Plaza Ernest Lluch ▪ 959 59 00 25 ▪ Open 10:30am–3pm, 4–7pm daily ▪ Adm ▪ www.parquemineroderiotinto.es

The Ríotinto (Red River) mines, the world's oldest, have been exploited for minerals for some 5,000 years, and the gradual stripping away of the rich ore has left a weird moonscape shot through with coloured fissures. A museum details the mines' history.

**Carmona and its castle tower**

### SOCIALISM VERSUS FEUDALISM

The fertile Campiña valley has been owned by a few noble families since the Catholic Monarchs handed out tracts as fiefdoms. The people who worked the land were little more than serfs, a situation that still accounts for local poverty. The mayor of Marinaleda, however, has created an island of social idealism, and has wrestled plots of property away from landlords to be communally owned by the workers.

**5 Carmona**
MAP C3 ■ Necrópolis: Avda Jorge Bonsor 9 ■ 600 14 36 32 ■ Open 9am–6pm Tue–Fri, 9:30am–2:30pm Sat & Sun ■ Closed public hols

The closest major town east of Seville has been continuously inhabited for more than 5,000 years. Its Roman remains are exceptional, especially the huge necropolis. The view from the originally Roman Puerta de Córdoba (Córdoba Gate) out over the sweeping plains also shouldn't be missed. Fine churches, palaces and *alcázares* adorn the site – one of the ancient castles is now a spectacular parador *(see p141)*.

**6 Cazalla de la Sierra**
MAP C3 ■ La Cartuja de Cazalla arts centre ■ 954 88 45 16 ■ Open daily ■ Adm

The main town in the Sierra Norte is a steep cluster of whitewashed houses. It's a popular place for weekend get-aways by *sevillanos* and particularly known for producing some of the area's famous anise-based tipples. Just 3 km (2 miles) outside of town is a former Carthusian monastery, restored as part hotel, part arts centre.

**7 Écija**
MAP D3 ■ Museo Histórico Municipal: Palacio de Benamejí, C/Cánovas del Castillo 4 ■ 955 90 29 19 ■ Opening times vary ■ Closed Mon ■ museo.ecija.es

Two nicknames for this town east of Seville give an idea of its chief glory and its biggest challenge. "The Town of Towers" refers to its 11 Baroque bell towers, all adorned with glazed tiles. "The Frying-Pan of Andalucía" alludes to its searing summer temperatures, due to the fact that it's one of the few towns not built on a hill. Écija's archaeological museum is worth a visit.

**8 Osuna**
MAP D4 ■ Colegiata: Plaza de la Encarnación ■ 954 81 04 44 ■ Open Jan–Mar & mid-Sep–Dec: 9am–6:30pm Tue–Sat (to 3:30pm Sun & hols); Apr–mid-Jun: 9am–8:30pm Tue–Fri (to 7pm Sat, 3:30pm Sun & hols); mid-Jun–mid-Sep: 9am–3:30pm Tue–Sun & hols ■ Adm

The powerful Dukes of Osuna get the credit for the exceptional architecture in this town. The huge Renaissance church, the Colegiata de la Asunción, dominates the scene; inside, there's a painting of the Crucifixion by José de Ribera. The University, also Renaissance, has tiled towers and a lovely central courtyard. Fine mansions also evoke the wealth of Spain's most powerful families *(see p50)*.

**Colegiata de la Asunción, Osuna**

### 9 Gruta de las Maravillas

MAP B3 ▪ C/Pozo de la Nieve, Aracena ▪ 663 93 78 76 ▪ Open 10am–1:30pm, 3–6pm daily ▪ Adm

A guided tour of these marvellous caves will wind through beautiful chambers with naturally coloured formations and names such as the Hut, Organ, Cathedral, Quail and Twins. The last room is a notorious crowd-pleaser – the *Sala de los Culos* (Chamber of the Buttocks). There are 12 caverns, and six underground lakes. The "Great Lake" lies under a vaulted ceiling, 70 m (230 ft) high.

**Inside the Gruta de las Maravillas**

### 10 Itálica

MAP B3 ▪ Avda de Extremadura 2, Santiponce ▪ 955 12 38 47 ▪ Open Apr–mid-Jun: 9am–8:30pm Tue–Sat, 9am–3:30pm Sun & hols; mid-Jun–mid-Sep: 9am–3:30pm Tue–Sun & hols; mid-Sep–Mar: 9am–6:30pm Tue–Sat, 9am–3:30pm Sun & hols ▪ Adm (free for EU members)

These wind-blown ruins were once the third-largest city in the Roman empire, founded in 206 BC and home to half a million people during the reign of Emperor Hadrian in the 2nd century. He was following in the glorious footsteps of his predecessor Trajan, another Itálica native. There's an amphitheatre and some mosaics amid the crumbling walls. Most of the wonders are still buried, or have been moved to the Archaeological Museum in Seville (see p86).

### A DAY IN COLUMBUS'S FOOTSTEPS

▶ **MORNING**

Head to the **Monasterio de Santa María de la Rábida**, 9 km (5.5 miles) from Huelva (see p95), where a despondent Columbus found spiritual solace and practical help from the prior. The latter persuaded Queen Isabel to sponsor the voyage that would discover America. The monks give tours (10am–1pm, 4–7pm Tue–Sun; winter to 6:15pm • Adm) showing Columbus's rooms.

On the waterfront below, la **Muelle de las Carabelas** sports replicas of the three boats that made the trip (see p70).

The café at the monastery is a pleasant place for lunch.

**AFTERNOON**

Some 4 km (2.5 miles) northeast of La Rábida is the port, **Palos de la Frontera**, from which Columbus set sail. The Iglesia de San Jorge is where the crew heard mass before departing. La Fontanilla, the well that supplied them with water, is behind the church.

A further 7 km (4 miles) northeast is **Moguer**. At the Convento de Santa Clara, Columbus gave thanks after his first voyage for having survived a storm in the Azores (Tours 10:30am, 11:30am, 12:30pm, 4:30pm, 5:30pm, 6:30pm Tue–Sat, 10:30am, 11:30am Sun • Adm).

Relax over a meal at La Parrala (Plaza de las Monjas 22 • 959 37 04 52 • Closed Mon • €€).

*See map on pp94–5*

# The Best of the Rest

 **Jabugo**
MAP B3

The "home of ham" produces Spain's most famous, known as *jamón ibérico* (cured Iberian ham), *jamón serrano* (mountain-cured ham) and *pata negra*, named after the black pigs that forage in the Sierra de Aracena.

**2 Niebla**
MAP B4

Massive ramparts, built by the Moors in the 12th century, attest to the central role this town played in defending the land. The walls stretch for about 2.5 km (1.5 miles).

**3 Sierra de Aracena y Picos de Aroche Park**
MAP B2

This wild area provides plenty of inspiring views and fauna *(see p60)*.

**4 Aroche**
MAP A2 ■ Museo del Santo Rosario: Paseo Ordoñez Valdés ■ 959 14 02 01 ■ Open mid-May–Sep: 11am–3pm Thu–Sun & public hols; Oct–mid-May: 10am–2pm & 3–5pm Fri–Sun & public hols

This well-preserved village contains a wonderful oddity, the Museo del Santo Rosario, packed with rosaries that have belonged to Mother Teresa, John F Kennedy and General Franco.

**5 Cortegana**
MAP B3

A 13th-century castle dominates one of the largest towns in the area.

**The town of Cortegana**

**6 Aracena**
MAP B3

Capital of the sierra, this is an attractive little town. The crumbling Castillo de Aracena offers sweeping views of the surrounding hills.

**7 Almonaster la Real**
MAP B3

A 10th-century mosque and castle, as well as a bullring, are clustered on a citadel overlooking the village *(see p56)*.

**The Mezquita at Almonaster la Real**

**8 Santa Olalla del Cala**
MAP B3

In the heart of the ham-curing area, this village has a 13th-century castle and a 15th-century Baroque church.

**9 Alájar**
MAP B3

A small town of cobbled streets and white-washed buildings *(see p56)*.

**10 Zufre**
MAP B3

This cliff-top community is like a mini-Ronda *(see pp30–31)*. The Paseo de los Alcaldes has rose and lime trees and views across the plain.

# Provincial Shopping

### 1 Aroche Markets
Thursday is the day the market stalls arrive in this Huelvan town. The market in Plaza de Abastos features a traditional produce spread, including the strong-flavoured goat's cheese favoured by the locals.

### 2 Souvenirs
In Aracena, head for the Calle Pozo de la Nieve, a cobbled street lined with souvenir shops. In El Rocío (see p95), souvenir stalls flank the church, hawking paraphernalia associated with the famous Romería pilgrimage (see p36).

### 3 Crafts
In addition to leather, Valverde del Camino is known for furniture and fine wooden boxes. Embroidery work from Aracena and Bollullos del Condado is worth seeking out, as well as linen tablecloths from Cortegana and Moguer. Wickerwork is widely sold around Huelva, while nearer the coast it is also common to see Moroccan goods for sale.

### 4 Pottery
In this area, pottery has traditional patterns influenced by Moorish art. Look for water jugs, plates and jars decorated in blue, green and white glazes.

### 5 Leather
The most notable leather goods come from Valverde del Camino. Choose *botos camperos* (cowboy boots) or the longer *botos rocieros* (Spanish riding boots). Many shops produce footwear, and a number of craftsmen make boots to order, taking three to four days to make a pair. There are workshops devoted to making saddles and bridles.

*Jamón ibérico* from Jabugo

### 6 Ham
The Mesón Sánchez Romero Carvajal in Jabugo is one of the top producers of the local *jamón ibérico*.

### 7 El Condado Wine District
The name refers to an area noted for its reliable white wine. Local *finos* include Condado Pálido and Condado Viejo.

### 8 Anise Liqueur
The liqueur of choice throughout the region is anise-based. One of the best is Anis Cazalla from the eponymous town (see p96).

**Local pottery**

### 9 Huelva
The provincial capital (see p95) boasts its own El Corte Inglés department store on Plaza de España, while the area around it and just off Plaza 12 de Octobre constitutes the main shopping district. The Mercadillo (open-air market) is held every Friday on the Recinto Colombino.

### 10 Cured Fish
Considered a great delicacy and priced accordingly, raw wind-cured tuna (*mojama*) is an acquired taste. Isla Cristina is the main centre of production, but you can buy it in the Mercado del Carmen in Huelva, and other food markets.

*See map on pp94–5*

# Cafés and Tapas Bars

**Hostería La Rábida**

### 1 Hostería La Rábida
MAP A4 ▪ Paraje de la Rábida ▪ 959 35 00 35 ▪ Closed Mon & Jan

Next to an old monastery, just east of Huelva where Columbus found spiritual retreat, you can have a drink or snack, or enjoy a full meal.

### 2 Bar Plaza, Carmona
MAP C3 ▪ Plaza San Fernando ▪ 954 19 00 67

In the heart of town, with an outdoor terrace, this is a great little place for tapas. The *montaditos* ("little sandwiches") are well worth a try. One of the specialities is the typical local dish *espinacas con garbanzos*, spinach with chickpeas.

### 3 El Martinete, Cazalla
MAP C3 ▪ Ctra Estación de Cazalla km12 ▪ 955 88 65 33 (information) ▪ Closed Mon

A tiny bar on a camp site so, along with good-value tapas, there are woods and waterfalls to enjoy.

### 4 Bar La Reja, Écija
MAP D3 ▪ C/Garcilópez 1 ▪ 954 83 30 12 ▪ Closed Sun & Mon

This local favourite offers a wide choice of tapas and *raciones* and the leisurely atmosphere invites lingering.

### 5 La Puerta Ancha, Ayamonte
MAP A4 ▪ Plaza de la Laguna 14 ▪ 959 32 06 66

A sociable place that purports to be the original town bar. There are tables on the square and good prices, too, for their line of drinks, tapas and other snacks.

### 6 Espuma del Mar, Isla Canela
MAP A4 ▪ Paseo de los Gavilanes 28 ▪ 959 47 72 85

This beachside establishment has alfresco tables and tasty tapas. The speciality is, of course, fresh fish and seafood. Try *raya* (skate) in one of its various manifestations.

### 7 El Refugio, Mazagón
MAP B4 ▪ Calle Santa Clara 43 ▪ 610 74 53 31 ▪ Closed Mon–Thu

A laid-back, popular haunt in this surfer's paradise. Located a short stroll from the beach, El Refugio is renowned for its fresh fish dishes.

### 8 Mesón La Reja, Aracena
MAP B3 ▪ Carretera N433 km87 ▪ 959 12 76 70

This tapas bar specializes in regional food including wild mushrooms, local cheeses and snails.

### 9 Café Bar Manzano, Aracena
MAP B3 ▪ Plaza del Marqués de Aracena 22 ▪ 959 12 81 23 ▪ Closed Tue, last week Sep

On the south side of the town square this traditional bar is a classic Sierra place for coffee and a pastry.

### 10 Casa Curro, Osuna
MAP D4 ▪ Plazuela Salitre 5 ▪ 955 82 07 58

A few blocks from the main square, this is a premier tapas bar. Worth seeking out for the quality.

*Patatas bravas*

# Restaurants

###  La Choza de Manuela, Bormujos

MAP B4 ▪ C/Menendez Pidal 2 ▪ 955 72 60 92 ▪ €

Popular with locals, this restaurant specializes in a variety of succulent, grilled meats, served by friendly staff. Go early to avoid the long queues.

### 2 Meson Rey Arturo, Osuna

MAP D4 ▪ C/Sor Angela 3 ▪ 662 13 22 21 ▪ Closed Mon–Wed, Sun D ▪ No credit cards ▪ €

The medieval decor in "The inn of King Arthur" does not disappoint. Feast on grilled meats and modern interpretations of regional classics.

### 3 Restaurante Miramar, Punta Umbría

MAP A4
▪ C/Miramar 1
▪ 959 31 12 43
▪ €

Fresh fish from the Atlantic is paired with rice dishes.

### 4 Restaurante Montecruz, Aracena

MAP B3 ▪ Plaza de San Pedro 36 ▪ 959 12 60 13 ▪ Closed Tue or Wed ▪ €€

Local, organic produce is key, with game, ham, chestnuts and wild mushrooms when in season. Exceptional food in both the restaurant and tapas bar.

### 5 Cambio de Tercio, Constantina

MAP C3 ▪ C/Virgen del Robledo 53 bajo, Constantina ▪ 955 88 10 80 ▪ Closed Tue, last week Sep ▪ €

This place is popular with devotees of rural cookery. Specialities include Iberian pork loin in wild mushroom sauce and for dessert *tarta de castañas* (chestnut tart).

**PRICE CATEGORIES**

For a three-course meal for one with half a bottle of wine (or equivalent meal), taxes and extra charges.

€ under €30  €€ €30–€50  €€€ over €50

### 6 Restaurante Azabache, Huelva

MAP A4 ▪ C/Vázquez López 22 ▪ 959 25 75 28 ▪ Closed Sat D, Sun ▪ €€€

A smart traditional eatery that's popular with locals (later in the evening) and is known for its *raciones*, or large servings of tapas.

### 7 Casa Luciano, Ayamonte

MAP A4 ▪ C/Palma del Condado 1 ▪ 959 47 10 71 ▪ Closed Sun D, Mon ▪ €

The place for fresh, tempting seafood and fish stews. Try the *atún al horno* (baked tuna) or grilled sardines.

**Fresh grilled sardines**

### 8 Aires de Doñana, El Rocío

MAP B4 ▪ Avda La Canaliega, 1 ▪ 959 44 22 89 ▪ Closed Mon, 20 days in July ▪ €€

French windows provide panoramic views of the marshes here. The "shack" specializes in local dishes. The suckling kid in aubergine sauce is a treat.

### 9 Posada de Cortegana, Cortegana

MAP A2 ▪ Ctra El Repilado – La Corte km 2.5 ▪ 959 50 33 17 ▪ €€

A wide variety of meat, such as Iberian pork, venison and game, is on offer at this lovely grillhouse.

### 10 Casa El Padrino, Alájar

MAP B3 ▪ Plaza Miguel Moya 2 ▪ 959 12 56 01 ▪ €

This rustic favourite is known for its tasty regional cuisine.

*See map on pp94–5* ←

# TOP10 Málaga and Cádiz Provinces

These two Andalucian provinces are a heady mix of cultural and recreational riches. Europe's oldest city, Cádiz, is found here, but the presence of history is balanced by the hedonistic delights of the Costa del Sol and its fine beaches. Some of the region's most dramatic landscapes lure nature-lovers, while others are drawn by the charms of the famed *pueblos blancos* (white villages), the most renowned being Ronda, birthplace of that strongest of Spanish traditions, the bullfight. This is also the area that produces the world-famous fortified wines known as *Jerez* (sherry), as well as the celebrated sweet wines of Málaga. Finally, Europe's southernmost point is located here, Tarifa, with views of North Africa, and a stone's throw away, the Rock of Gibraltar.

**Statue outside Ronda's bullring**

## AREA MAP OF MÁLAGA AND CÁDIZ PROVINCES

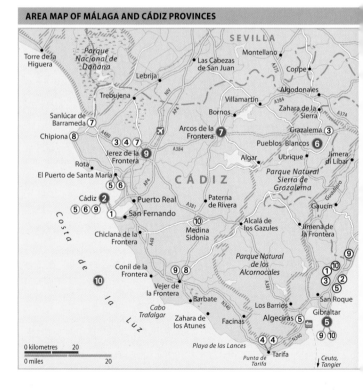

**Puento Nuevo, Ronda**

## 1 Ronda

To many visitors over the centuries, this town evokes the "real" Andalucía, wild and spectacular. This mountain rock eyrie is breathtaking, being dramatically sliced down the middle by El Tajo, a fantastically deep and narrow limestone ravine, formed over thousands of years by the Río Guadalevín. Thus Ronda is a town of two halves – the ancient half is steeped in rich Moorish history, with cobbled streets, while the more modern part is on the north side *(see pp30–31)*.

## 2 Cádiz

At the apex of the Atlantic's untamed Costa de la Luz *(see p106)*, ancient Cádiz floats on what was originally its own island. It is possibly Europe's oldest city, thought to have been founded by the Phoenicians in around 1104 BC. Much of what can be seen today, however, dates from the 18th century – the city was destroyed by an Anglo-Dutch raid in 1596. Catedral Nueva (1722) is one of Spain's largest churches, and many Baroque edifices enhance this unpretentiously beautiful provincial capital. Apart from two weeks in February when Cádiz stages Spain's most celebrated Carnaval *(see p80)*, it remains under-visited *(see pp26–7)*.

| | | |
|---|---|---|
| **1** Top 10 Sights *see pp103–6* | **1** Costa del Sol Nightlife *see p110* |
| **1** Costa del Sol Places to Eat *see p111* | **1** Nightlife in the Region *see p112* |
| **1** Places to Eat in the Region *see p113* | **1** The Best of the Rest *see p107* |
| | **1** Costa del Sol Golf Courses *see p109* |

**Roman amphitheatre, Málaga**

Málaga's alcázar, built between the 8th and 11th centuries, includes a Roman amphitheatre.

### 3 Málaga

MAP E5 ■ Museo Picasso: C/San Agustín 8 ■ 952 12 76 00 ■ Open daily, check website for details ■ Adm ■ www.museopicassomalaga.org

Despite being home to the main airport bringing holidaymakers to the Costa del Sol, this provincial capital has been bypassed by the brunt of "sun coast" development and has managed to hold onto its Spanish-ness quite admirably. It has a thriving arts scene and attracts foodies to its many restaurants. The modern waterfront complex has shops, bars, a promenade and space for plush yachts. Important as a trading port since ancient times, it was the favourite city of poet García Lorca (see p49), who loved its rawness. But its even greater claim to artistic fame is that it was the birthplace of Pablo Picasso, whose creative genius is celebrated in the Picasso museum, which opened in 2003 (see p54).

### 4 Antequera

MAP D4 ■ Museo Municipal: Palacio Nájera, Plaza del Coso Viejo ■ 952 70 83 00 ■ Open Tue–Sun ■ Adm

So ancient that even the Romans called it Antiquaria, this market town presents a wonderfully condensed architectural history of the entire area, beginning with Neolithic dolmens dating from between 4500 and 2500 BC. In addition, there are significant Roman ruins, including villas with outstanding mosaics, a Moorish Alcazaba (closed to the public), the 16th-century Arco de los Gigantes and fine Renaissance palaces and churches to explore. Many treasures originally found in the town – including the exquisite Ephebe of Antequera, a rare, life-size Roman bronze statue of a young boy – are displayed in the Municipal Museum, housed in an 18th-century palace.

### 5 Gibraltar

MAP C6

This gargantuan chunk of limestone rising up from the Mediterranean was one of the mythic Pillars of Hercules. Yet, despite being nick-named "The Rock", as a worldwide symbol of stability and security, this fortress is actually a serious political

**The Rock of Gibraltar**

football these days. Taken by the English in 1704 during the War of the Spanish Succession, today it is still very much a part of the British ethos, and only grudgingly do the Spaniards who live around it even acknowledge its existence. The Spanish government meanwhile most definitely wants it back. Legend has it that Britain will retain sovereignty of the rock as long as its most famous residents, the wild Barbary apes, remain, but their increasing number does not prevent ongoing diplomatic arguments. If you're homesick for Englishness, cross over the frontier at La Línea to enjoy fish and chips or a pint of ale.

Casares, a pretty *pueblo blanco*

### 6 Pueblos Blancos
MAP C5

The term "white villages" refers to the profusion of whitewashed hillside hamlets in the Serranía de Ronda, the mountainous territory around Ronda. Many are truly beautiful and it's well worth spending several days driving from one to the other, and then striking out on foot to take in some of the views *(see p69)*. Towns not to miss include Gaucín, Casares, Grazalema, Setenil, Zahara de la Sierra, Jimena de Libár and Manilva. Villagers, who originally settled here to protect themselves from bandits in the lowlands, retain a centuries-old way of life and strong agricultural tradition. Between Grazalema and Zahara, you'll go through Andalucía's highest mountain pass, the breath-taking Puerto de las Palomas (The Pass of the Doves).

### A MORNING WALK IN JEREZ DE LA FRONTERA

▶ MORNING

Begin your tour at the impressive **Alcázar**, with its many Moorish remains, including restored gardens, a mosque and a *hammam* (baths), as well as a *camera obscura* providing views of the city and beyond. Beside it is the stunningly decorated **cathedral**, extravagantly rich inside and out. Note the fine painting of *The Sleeping Girl* by Zurbarán in the sacristy.

Next take the tour – with tastings – of the **González-Byass bodega** *(see p76)*, featuring possibly the oldest cellars in Jerez, with one designed by Gustave Eiffel. Don't miss the many signatures of famous people on the barrels (called "butts"), including Queen Victoria, Cole Porter, Martin Luther King and General Franco, among others.

Continuing on north, the **Pedro Domecq bodega** *(see p76)* also offers tours and is distinctively Moorish in style. A block further north, pop into the **Museo Arqueológico** to see the prized Greek bronze helmet from the 7th century BC, and then enter the **Barrio de Santiago**. This gently dilapidated neighbourhood of maze-like alleyways is home to a sizeable gypsy community and numerous flamenco venues.

To cap off your walk, continue southeast out of the *barrio*, past the **Church of San Dionisio**, to **Reino de León** on Calle Latorre *(see page 113)*, Jerez's top-rated, wildly inventive tapas bar.

*See map on pp102–3* ←

### 7 Arcos de la Frontera

MAP C5 ▪ Galería de Arte Arx-Arcis: C/Marqués de Torresoto 11 ▪ 956 70 39 51 ▪ Open 10:30am–8:30pm daily

Another town built atop a sheer cliff, this is probably the most dazzling of the *pueblos blancos* and the one situated furthest west. Little remains of the period before the *reconquista*, when it received its "de la Frontera" appellation, as a bastion "on the frontier" between Christian and Moorish Spain. The Galería de Arte Arx-Arcis crafts museum and shop displays local carpets, blankets, baskets and pottery.

### 8 The Costa del Sol

This string of former Mediterranean fishing villages still lives up to its reputation as one of the world centres for sun, surf and fun. But beyond the brash tourist enclaves there is much authentic charm on offer and even places that invite tranquility – especially in the towns of Estepona, Nerja, Mijas and ultra-classy Marbella (*see p65*). Year-round golf makes the whole area a great attraction for international fans of the sport (*see p109*) and, in high

Nerja beach, Costa del Sol

season in particular, Torremolinos is the place to find some of Spain's liveliest nightlife (*see p33*).

### 9 Jerez de la Frontera

MAP B5 ▪ Alcázar de Jerez: Calle Alameda Vieja ▪ 956 14 99 55 ▪ Open Apr–Jun, 16–30 Sep & Oct: 9:30am–5:30pm; Jul–15 Sep: to 7:30pm; Nov–Mar: to 2:30pm ▪ Adm

The largest city in Cádiz Province is synonymous with "sherry", which is a corruption of "Jerez" – itself a corruption of the Phoenician name of Xeres (*see p76–7*). Before that, it was part of the fabled Tartessian civilization (8th century BC). Sights include Jerez's Moorish fortress, once part of a 4-km (2.5-mile) wall (*see p105*). A well-preserved mosque, now the Santa María La Real chapel, features an octagonal cupola over the *mihrab* (prayer niche). Jerez is renowned for equestrian art, Andalucian style, as well as for flamenco (*see pp46–7*).

### 10 The Costa de la Luz

MAP B5–C6

Named for its shimmering sunlight (*luz*), the stretch of coast from Huelva down to Tarifa is all the things the Costa del Sol is not; its low-key resorts attract mainly Spanish visitors and water-sports lovers – the latter drawn by the strong ocean breezes. But there are plenty of pretty beaches, many backed by shady pine forests, and the combination of Arabic forts, Moorish castles, medieval churches, sherry and old-school charm makes the Costa de la Luz a great choice for adventurous holidaymakers.

---

**THE SHERRY TRIANGLE**

Jerez, Sanlúcar de Barrameda and El Puerto de Santa María mark the famed "Sherry Triangle". Production of the fortified wine (**above**) was started by the Phoenicians using vines they imported some 3,000 years ago. In Roman times it was exported all over the empire, and it has been popular in England since the Elizabethan age. Sherry varies in degrees of dryness or sweetness. The *fino* and *manzanilla* are dry and light, while the *amontillado* and *oloroso* are more robust (*see p77*).

# The Best of the Rest

###  1 El Chorro
MAP D4

A geographical wonder, the Chorro Gorge's immense gaping chasm, 180-m (590-ft) high, was created by the Río Guadalorce slashing through the limestone mountain. A 7.7 km (4.7 mile) long path, the Caminito del Rey, runs along the gorge.

### 2 El Torcal de Antequera
MAP D4

A mountain nature reserve, great for hiking. The bizarre limestone rock formations are the big draw *(see p60)*.

**El Caminito del Rey**

### 3 Grazalema
MAP C5

Nestled in the foothills of the Sierra del Pinar, Grazalema is a charming village – Spain's rainiest, according to some – and the main access point for the Sierra de Grazalema Natural Park, one of the best hiking areas in Andalucía *(see p60)*. Known for its local cheeses, stews and honey, it's also a great place to plan a picnic.

### 4 Tarifa
MAP C6

Possibly Andalucía's hippest coastal town, it has a sizable windsurfing and kitesurfing contingent *(see p64 & p66)* and a distinctly Moorish air.

### 5 Algeciras
MAP C6

Although the town of Algeciras is industrial and polluted, its port is the best in Spain; from here you can catch the ferry to Morocco. Peruse the Moorish bazaars while waiting for the boat to take you across.

### 6 El Puerto de Santa María
MAP B5

One of the Sherry Triangle towns. Several *bodegas* can be visited for tours and tastings *(see p76)*.

### 7 Sanlúcar de Barrameda
MAP B5

Famed for its *manzanilla* sherry and superb seafood, the town also offers beautiful churches, palaces and tours of the *bodegas*.

### 8 Chipiona
MAP B5

This pretty resort town is crowded with Spanish beach enthusiasts in high season. The pace of life is leisurely, consisting of enjoying the surf and miles of golden sand during the day, then strolls and ice cream until late in the evening.

### 9 Vejer de la Frontera
MAP C6

Of all the *pueblos blancos (see p105)*, this one has kept its Moorish roots most intact. Its original four Moorish gates still stand and its streets have barely changed in 1,000 years.

### 10 Medina Sidonia
MAP C5 ▪ Iglesia de Santa María la Coronada: Plaza Iglesia Mayor ▪ 956 41 03 29 ▪ Hours vary, call ahead for opening times ▪ Adm

The most important edifice here is the 15th-century church of Santa María la Coronada, built over an earlier mosque. The interior features a 15-m (50-ft) high *retablo*.

*See map on pp102–3*

# Provincial Shopping

 **Málaga Wines**
MAP Q5 ■ El Templo del Vino:
C/de Sebastián Souvirón 11, Málaga
■ 952 21 75 03

The region is famed for its sweet
wines (see p77), and Málaga has
plenty of establishments where they
can be sampled and purchased. El
Templo del Vino is particularly well
stocked with local tipples and also
with wines from all over Spain.

**Delicacies in a Málaga grocer**

 **Chocolates Artesanales Frigiliana**
MAP E5 ■ C/ Real 27, Frigiliana
■ 669 20 90 56

Set in a picturesque village, this
store sells over 15 unique chocolate
flavours and a range of cosmetics, all
made with a natural chocolate base.

 **Alegrías de Cádiz, Cádiz**
MAP B5 ■ Fabio Rufino 5
■ 956 06 87 09

This gourmet shop boasts an array
of wine, cheese, ham, pâté, olive oil,
marmalade, sweets and other
delicacies of the region.

 **Xauen, Conil de la Frontera**
MAP B5 ■ Calle Rafael Alberti 2, Conil
de la Frontera ■ 661 27 14 30

Shop specialising in a range of expertly
crafted leather goods, including
wallets, bags and bracelets.

 **Flamenco Costumes**
MAP B5 ■ Tamara Flamenco:
C/Santa Maria 5, Jerez ■ 956 34 74 89

Jerez is one of the very best places
to find genuine flamenco gear.

 **Equestrian Equipment**
MAP B5 ■ Hipisur: C/Circo 1,
Jerez ■ 956 32 42 09
■ www.hipisur.com

Jerez has to be one of the best
places in the world to find refined
horse-riding gear. Hipisur has an
extensive range of clothing and kit.

 **Sherry**
Jerez de la Frontera is, of
course, also the prime spot to
savour the finer points of a *fino*,
a *manzanilla*, an *amontillado* or an
*oloroso*. Tasting tours are available
at most *bodegas* (see pp76–7).

 **Traditional Textiles**
The villages of Grazalema and
Arcos de la Frontera (see pp106–7)
are known for their blankets, ponchos,
rugs and other woven textiles.

**Shopping in Gibraltar**
MAP C6

The shopping draw here is twofold:
there's no sales tax and it's mostly
duty-free. Several UK high-street
names are represented, such as The
Body Shop and Marks & Spencer.

**Leather**
In the shops of Ronda (see
pp30–31) you'll find some of the best
prices on leather goods of anywhere
in Spain. Many of the items have
well-known labels, since fashion
houses often have contracts with
leather factories in this area.

**Shopping in Ronda**

# Costa del Sol Golf Courses

 **Valderrama**
MAP C6 ■ Avda los Cortijos, s/n San Roque ■ 956 79 12 00 ■ www.valderrama.com

The most famous golf club along the Costa, it has hosted the Ryder Cup and is a Robert Trent Jones masterpiece.

**Lush greens on Valderrama golf course**

**2 Real Club de Golf Sotogrande**
MAP D6 ■ Paseo del Parque, Sotogrande ■ 956 78 50 14 ■ www.golfsotogrande.com

Royal Sotogrande opened in 1964 and is still one of Europe's top 10 courses. Green-fee-paying visitors are welcome if they book in advance. The Robert Trent Jones design features mature trees and water obstacles.

**3 San Roque**
MAP C6 ■ N340 km126.5, San Roque ■ 956 61 30 30 ■ www.sanroqueclub.com

Opened in 1990, San Roque is a Dave Thomas design. The course has been planned so that the holes are located in the same direction as the prevailing wind.

**4 Real Club Las Brisas**
MAP D5 ■ Urbanización Nueva Calle Londres 1 (Andalucía), above Puerto Banús, Marbella ■ 952 81 30 21 ■ www.realclubdegolflasbrisas.com

Recognized as one of the finest courses in Europe, this was also designed by Robert Trent Jones. The grounds boast raised greens, sand traps and water features. Opened in 1968, it has hosted the World Cup twice and the Spanish Open three times.

**5 Alcaidesa Links**
MAP C6 ■ N340 km124.6, La Línea ■ 956 79 10 40 ■ www.alcaidesagolf.com

The only links course in Spain, Alcaidesa opened in 1992, designed by Peter Alliss and Clive Clark.

**6 Golf El Paraíso**
MAP D5 ■ Ctra N340, km167, Estepona ■ 952 88 38 35 ■ www.elparaisogolf.com

This British-style golf venue was designed by Gary Player.

**7 Los Arqueros**
MAP D5 ■ Ctra de Ronda A397 km44.5, Benahavis ■ 952 78 46 00 ■ www.losarquerosgolf.com

The Costa's first course to be designed by Seve Ballesteros is a tough test.

**8 Miraflores**
MAP D5 ■ Urbanización Riviera del Sol, Ctra de Cadiz km198, Calle Severiano Ballesteros ■ 952 93 19 60 ■ www.miraflores-golf.com

Folco Nardi's design has many challenging holes.

**9 La Duquesa**
MAP D5 ■ Urbanización El Hacho, N340 km143, Manilva ■ 952 89 07 25 ■ www.golfladuquesa.com

A Trent Jones design, the front nine holes begin in a westerly direction then finish with a long par five.

**10 La Cañada**
MAP C6 ■ Ctra Guadiaro km1, Guadiaro, San Roque ■ 956 79 41 00 ■ www.lacanadagolf.com

The long 1st hole sets the tone for a tough round – the 4th offers no view of the green until the third shot.

*See map on pp102–3*

# Costa del Sol Nightlife

 **Ocean Club, Marbella**
MAP D5 ▪ Avda Lola Flores
▪ 952 90 81 37

A chic club featuring a saltwater swimming pool and a VIP area with huge round beds.

**② Suite, Marbella**
MAP D5 ▪ Puente Romano Hotel, Bulevar Príncipe Alfonso von Hohenlohe, Ctra de Cádiz km177

This beachfront club has huge Buddhas, fire-eaters, belly dancers and jugglers. In the summer, the club becomes Suite del Mar and moves beachside among palm trees.

**③ Club de Jazz y Cócteles Speakeasy, Fuengirola**
MAP D5 ▪ Centro Comercial Las Rampas, Local 10 ▪ 656 48 79 19

Styled after the speakeasies of the 1920s, this bar has live jazz music at weekends and great cocktails.

**④ Cavalli Club, Marbella**
MAP D5 ▪ Ctra de Cádiz, km175
▪ 603 50 86 42

Based in the Puerto Banús marina, this large nightclub has several areas, including a VIP penthouse and an alfresco dance floor. Nights are hosted by DJs from all over Europe.

**⑤ Olivia Valère, Marbella**
MAP D5 ▪ Ctra de Istán, km0.8
▪ 952 82 88 61

This exclusive club is a Costa hot spot. Designed by the same creative genius who did Paris's famous Buddha Bar, it attracts the rich and beautiful.

**Olivia Valère – a Costa hot spot**

**⑥ Puerto Marina, Benalmádena**
MAP D5 ▪ Puerto Marina

A large complex with a variety of bars, nightclubs, shops and eateries.

**⑦ Mango, Benalmádena**
MAP D5 ▪ Plaza Solymar

Popular with the younger crowds, this club has an electric atmosphere and throbbing, alternative music.

**Slot machines, Casino Torrequebrada**

**⑧ Casino Torrequebrada, Benalmádena**
MAP D5 ▪ Avda del Sol ▪ 952 57 73 00
▪ www.casinotorrequebrada.com

Located in the Hotel Torrequebrada, the casino has tables for blackjack, chemin de fer, punto y banco and roulette. The nightclub offers a flamenco show. Smart dress.

**⑨ La Taberna de Pepe Lopez, Torremolinos**
MAP E5 ▪ Plaza de la Gamba Alegre
▪ 952 38 12 84 ▪ Closed Sun

This flamenco venue is highly touristy, but fun. Shows take place here between 10pm and midnight.

**⑩ Gay Torremolinos**
MAP E5

Torremolinos has the best gay nightlife on the Costa del Sol. Start at terrace bar El Gato (Paseo Marítimo Antonio Machado 1), then try Parthenon (Calle Nogalera) with its two dance floors. Centuryon (Calle Casablanca 15) is the biggest gay club outside Madrid or Barcelona.

# Costa del Sol Places to Eat

### 1 La Pappardella, Marbella
MAP D5 ■ Muelle de Honor
■ 952 81 50 89 ■ €€

Enjoy true Neapolitan cuisine at this family-orientated eatery with a wide range of pasta, pizza and seafood.

### 2 El Tintero II, Málaga
MAP E5 ■ Ctra Almería 99, Playa del Dedo ■ 952 20 68 26
■ Disabled access ■ €

An open-air fish restaurant on the beach. There's no menu – the waiter will tell you what's on offer.

### 3 El Estrecho, Marbella
MAP D5 ■ C/San Lázaro 12
■ 952 77 00 04 ■ Closed first 2 weeks in Jun & Christmas ■ €

Another winning tapas bar and local favourite. There's a terrace, seafood treats and nice *fino*. Try the *boquerones al limón* (anchovies in lemon).

### 4 La Sirena, Benalmádena
MAP D5 ■ Paseo Maritimo
■ 952 56 02 39 ■ Disabled access ■ €

On the beachfront, and the paella is one of the best in the area.

### 5 Bodegas Quitapenas, Torremolinos
MAP E5 ■ C/Cuesta del Tajo 3
■ 952 38 62 44 ■ No credit cards ■ €

An excellent tapas bar with Spanish seafood, including *pulpo* (octopus).

### 6 Restaurante La Escalera, Torremolinos
MAP E5 ■ C/Cuesta del Tajo 12
■ 952 05 80 24 ■ Closed Sun
■ Disabled access ■ €

A great little choice with dreamy terrace views. The international menu includes curry soup with peas.

### 7 Tapeo de Cervantes, Málaga
MAP E5 ■ C/Cárcer 8 ■ 952 60 94 58
■ Closed Sun L, Mon ■ Disabled access ■ €€

This charming, rustic *bodega* serves hearty regional food with some novel touches. Try the *estofado de cordero* (lamb stew with mint and couscous).

### 8 Bar Altamirano, Marbella
MAP D5 ■ Plaza Altamirano 3
■ 952 82 49 32 ■ Closed Wed, mid-Jan–mid-Feb ■ €

Despite Marbella's glitzy image there are affordable, traditional tapas bars. This is one of them, just southeast of Plaza Naranjos; seafood specialities are listed on ceramic menus.

**Alfresco dining at Bar Altamirano**

### 9 Restaurante 34, Nerja
MAP E5 ■ Calle Hernando de Carabeo 34 ■ 952 52 54 44 ■ €€€

Cut into the cliff, the café gives views of the sea while you are protected under palm frond umbrellas.

### 10 Lan Sang, Nerja
MAP E5 ■ C/Malaga 12
■ 952 52 80 53 ■ Closed Sun L, Mon
■ Disabled access ■ €€

For a change of cuisine, try this Thai/Laotian restaurant. The modern, elegant decor is matched by the sophisticated flavours and beautiful presentation of the food.

*See map on pp102–3*

# Nightlife in the Region

An evening out in Nerja

### ① Nerja by Night
MAP E5
■ Jimmy's: C/Antonio Millán 2
■ Discoteca People: C/Chaparil

If you're looking for nightlife in Nerja, head to Plaza Tutti Frutti where there are around 25 bars and nightspots offering everything from cocktails to karaoke. Nearby are two of the best-known clubs: Jimmy's and Discoteca People. Beware of pickpockets.

### ② Barsovia, Málaga
MAP R4 ■ C/Mendez Nuñez 3

This old-town disco attracts people of all ages. The music is a mix of 1980s feel-good, with some current hits thrown in.

### ③ ZZ Pub, Málaga
MAP Q4 ■ C/Tejón y Rodríguez 6

Mostly students come to this modest establishment in the old town to hear the bands that play here on Mondays and Thursdays. A DJ fills in the quiet moments every night.

### ④ Tarifa
MAP C6 ■ Almedina Tarifa: C/Almedina ■ Café del Mar: Poligonal Industrial La Vega

Almedina Tarifa is one of the oldest and most beautiful bars in town, with flamenco on Thursday nights. Nightclub Café del Mar has three floors including a roof terrace.

### ⑤ Cádiz
MAP B5
■ Sala Anfiteatro: Paseo Pascual Pery Junquera
■ 956 22 45 19

The zone around the harbour is loaded with venues and Anfiteatro is one of the best. Open Thursday to Saturday.

### ⑥ Flamenco in Cádiz
MAP B5 ■ Peña La Perla: C/Carlos Ollero ■ Peña Enrique el Mellizo: Punta San Felipe, C/Nuevo Mundo 1

The flamenco clubs burst with life in Cádiz. Good bets include Peña La Perla and Peña Enrique el Mellizo.

### ⑦ Flamenco in Jerez
MAP B5

Here you will find genuine flamenco at its impassioned best. The gypsy quarter of Santiago is the place to make for, where you will find a number of *peñas* (clubs), but don't expect much before 10pm.

### ⑧ Ronda
MAP D5 ■ Café Las Bridas: C/Remedios 18 ■ Café Pub Dulcinea: C/Rios Rosas 3

Café Las Bridas offers imported brews, with live music on weekends from midnight. Dance to Spanish electro-pop at Café Pub Dulcinea.

### ⑨ Gibraltar
MAP C6

There are more than 360 pubs in Gibraltar. If you enjoy late nights you should visit Queensway Quay, Marina Bay and Casemates Square, which have a wide selection of bars, often with live entertainment.

### ⑩ Gambling in Gibraltar
MAP C6 ■ Ocean Village

In addition to its lively bar scene, the Rock boasts the Gala Casino, which has spectacular views over the bay.

# Places to Eat in the Region

**PRICE CATEGORIES**

For a three-course meal for one with half a bottle of wine (or equivalent meal), taxes and extra charges.

€ under €30 ▪ €€ €30–€50 ▪ €€€ over €50

### 1 Ventorrillo del Chato, Cádiz

MAP B5 ▪ Ctra Cádiz-San Fernando 2km (Via Augusta Julia) ▪ 956 25 00 25 ▪ Closed Sun D ▪ €€

The oldest restaurant in Cádiz (1780) is also one of the best. Try *salmorejo*, a thick tomato soup served as a dip or side dish, and *dorada a la sal*, a local fish baked in a salt crust.

### 2 Antigua Casa de Guardia, Málaga

MAP Q5 ▪ Alameda Principal 18 ▪ 952 21 46 80 ▪ Closed Sun ▪ €

The city's oldest *taberna*, dating from 1840, has barrels of local wine in the bar. The steamed mussels are great.

**Wine in Antigua Casa de Guardia**

### 3 Reino de León, Jerez

MAP B5 ▪ C/Latorre 8 ▪ 956 32 29 15 ▪ €€

Chic modern eatery. The inventive menu includes *arancini* with whole prawns and fish with fruit caviar.

### 4 Bar Juanito, Jerez

MAP B5 ▪ C/Pescadería Vieja 8 & 10 ▪ 956 34 12 18 ▪ Closed Sun D ▪ €

Famous for the best tapas in town. It closes during the Feria in May.

### 5 Casa Flores, El Puerto de Santa María

MAP B5 ▪ C/Ribera del Río 9 ▪ 956 54 35 12 ▪ €€

A stunning setting and the finest fresh seafood make this one of the best choices in this port town.

### 6 Sollo, Fuengirola

MAP D5 ▪ Avenida del Higuerón 48 ▪ 951 38 56 22 ▪ Closed L ▪ €€€

Chef Diego Gallegos serves up unusual tapas-style dishes using snail caviar, eels, trout ceviche and ox-steak – all beautifully presented.

**Caviar at Sollo**

### 7 TragaTapas, Ronda

MAP D5 ▪ C/Nueva 4 ▪ 952 87 72 09 ▪ €€

Friendly, trendy and popular with Ronda residents. Former El Bulli chef Benito Gómez creates some of the best tapas in Andalucía. Stocks local Schatz organic wines.

### 8 Jardín del Califa, Vejer de la Frontera

MAP C6 ▪ Plaza de España 16 ▪ 956 45 17 06 ▪ Closed Sun ▪ €€€

Truly exquisite North African and Middle Eastern cuisine is served in an enchanting complex of medieval buildings. Dine in the shady garden or a stone vaulted cellar.

### 9 Balandro, Cádiz

MAP B5 ▪ Alameda Apodaca 22 ▪ 956 22 09 92 ▪ €€

In an 18th-century mansion overlooking the bay, Balandro serves superb fried and grilled fish.

### 10 De Locos Tapas, Ronda

MAP D5 ▪ C/Arquitecto Pons Sorolla, 7 ▪ 951 08 37 72 ▪ Closed Sun, Mon ▪ €€

Worth the walk for its tapas. Try the daily specials using seasonal foods.

*See map on pp102–3* ←

# TOP10 Granada and Almería Provinces

Seduced by the photogenic fantasy that is the Alhambra, tourists often forget to make time to see the area's other attractions. Besides Granada's many religious and cultural landmarks, the entire region is worth exploring. Hikers will enjoy the mountain trails of the Sierra Nevada, beach-lovers will discover still unspoilt coastal areas and fans of Spaghetti Westerns will marvel at desert locations and movie film sets.

**Urn, Cueva-Museo, Guadix**

## 1 Guadix

MAP F4 ▪ Cueva-Museo: Plaza Padre Poveda ▪ 958 66 47 67 ▪ Open 10:30am–2pm, 4:30–8pm daily ▪ Adm ▪ www.cuevamuseo alcazaba.com

This ancient town is famous for its cave dwellings, inhabited for centuries. They were developed after the *reconquista* by local Moors who had been cast out of society by the Christians. The Barrio de las Cuevas is a surreal zone of brown hills with rounded whitewashed chimneys sprouting up here and there. To learn more, visit the Cueva-Museo or stay in a cave hotel *(see p146)*.

## 2 Cathedral and Capilla Real, Granada

MAP Q2 ▪ Catedral: C/Gran Vía de Colón 5; open 10am–6:30pm Mon–Sat, 2:30–6:30pm Sun & hols; adm ▪ Capilla Real: C/Oficios 3; 958 22 78 48; opening times vary, check website for details; adm; www. capillarealgranada.com

To unequivocally establish Christian rule, these triumphalist structures were built by some of the greatest architects of the age. The interior of Granada's cathedral is one of the most stunning achievements, while Alonso Cano's façade echoes the ancient triple arch favoured by Roman

## AREA MAP OF GRANADA AND ALMERÍA PROVINCES

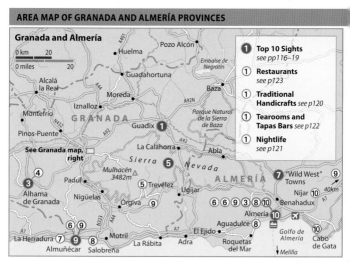

emperors. The Capilla Real (Royal Chapel) is Granada's finest Christian building and a repository of rare treasures, including a *reja* (gilded grille) by Bartolomé de Jaén, priceless jewels and paintings by Roger van der Weyden and Sandro Botticelli (*see p53*).

### ③ Alhama de Granada
MAP E4

Clinging precariously to the edge of a breathtaking gorge, the whitewashed village was known in Moorish times for its beauty and natural thermal waters (*al-hamma* means "hot spring" in Arabic). Hotel Balneario preserves an 11th-century *aljibe* (cistern), graced by Caliphal arches. In the 16th-century Iglesia de la Encarnación, some of the vestments are said to have been embroidered by Queen Isabel the Catholic.

### ④ Moorish Granada
■ MAP Q2 ■ Museo CajaGRANADA: Memoria de Andalucía, Avda de la Ciencia 2 ■ 958 22 22 57 ■ Open Sep–Jun: 9:30am–2pm Tue–Sat (also 4–7pm Thu–Sat), 11am–3pm Sun & hols; Jul: 9am–3pm Mon–Sat, 11am–3pm Sun & hols ■ Closed 1 & 6 Jan, 28 Feb, 1 May, 6, 24, 25 & 31 Dec ■ Adm ■ www.memoriadeandalucia.com

The fairy-tale palace of the Alhambra draws millions of visitors each year. In the city below, the ancient Albaicín district embodies a microcosm of a North African village, a "Little Morocco", with colourful market streets and tearooms. Behind the area stands Sacromonte, the traditional home of cave-dwelling gypsies. Also worth a visit is the Museo CajaGRANADA, devoted to Andalucian culture (*see pp12–17*).

**The magnificent Alhambra overlooking Granada**

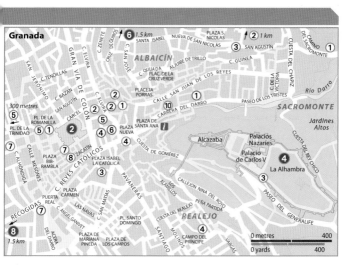

**Late-winter skiing in the Sierra Nevada mountains**

### ⑤ Sierra Nevada

Spain's tallest peaks – and, after the Alps, Europe's second-loftiest chain – make Andalucía home to some excellent winter sports and robust trekking in spring and summer, as well as abundant wild flowers and wildlife. For the more culturally inclined, the historic villages of the Alpujarras, on the southern slopes, are a fascinating study in an age-old way of life of the Sierra Nevada *(see pp38–9)*.

**Monasterio de la Cartuja, Granada**

### ⑥ Monasterio de la Cartuja, Granada

MAP F4 ■ Paseo de la Cartuja ■ 958 16 19 32 ■ Open 10am–1pm, 4–8pm (3–6pm in winter) daily ■ Adm

Don't let the austere exterior fool you – inside the church and sacristy of this Carthusian monastery lurks some of the most flamboyant Spanish Baroque detailing you'll ever encounter. So busy are the flourishes and arabesques of polychromed and gilded stucco that the architectural lines are all but swallowed up in ravishing visual commotion.

### ⑦ "Wild West" Towns

MAP G4 ■ Fort Bravo: Ctra N340 km 468, Paraje de Unihay, Tabernas; 902 07 08 14; open 9am–8pm; adm; fortbravooficial.com ■ Mini Hollywood: Ctra N340 km 464, Tabernas; 950 36 52 36; open 10am–6pm daily (summer), 10am–6pm Sat–Sun (winter); adm; www.oasysparque tematico.com ■ Western Leone: Ctra A92 km 378, Tabernas; 950 16 54 05; open 10am–8pm daily; adm; www. western-leone.es

The interior of Almería Province resembles the deserts and canyons of the American Southwest: it was the perfect spot for filming the Wild West epics known as "Spaghetti Westerns" of the 1960s and 1970s. Three of the sets are now theme parks: Mini Hollywood *(see p71)*, Fort Bravo and Western Leone offer stunt shows and memorabilia.

### ⑧ Museo Parque de las Ciencias

MAP F4 ■ Avda de la Ciencia, Granada ■ 958 13 19 00 ■ Open 10am–7pm Tue–Sat, 10am–3pm Sun & hols ■ Adm ■ www.parqueciencias.com

This exciting complex, dedicated to science and exploration, is made up of numerous interactive areas, such as Journey Through the Human Body, Perception, Eureka and Biosphere. There's an Observation Tower, a Planetarium and the Sala Explora, exclusively for children aged 3–7, where they can conduct their first experiments. There are temporary exhibitions too *(see p55)*.

## PLASTICULTURA

If you approach the coastal area of these provinces from the west, you will notice the extent of plastic tenting, a phenomenon that reaches a peak before Almería. This agricultural technique is known as *plasticultura* and squeezes out every drop of moisture from these desert lands in order to produce crops. The process is anything but organic, but this huge agribusiness does provide jobs.

### 9 Almuñécar and Around

MAP F5 ▪ Museo Arqueológico Cueva de Siete Palacios: Barrio de San Miguel ▪ 958 63 11 25 ▪ Open 10am–1:30pm & 4–6:30pm Tue–Sat, 10am–1pm Sun & public hols ▪ Adm

The Costa Tropical is a spectacular coast with towering mountains rising from the shore. Almuñécar is the chief town on this stretch and it is almost entirely devoted to resort life. Yet it has an ancient heritage, dating back to the Phoenicians, and was an important port under the Moors. The intriguing archaeological museum has a unique Egyptian vase dating from the 7th century BC.

**Alcazaba, Almería**

### 10 Almería and Around

MAP G4 ▪ Alcazaba: C/Almanzor ▪ 950 80 10 08 ▪ Open Tue–Sun; call ahead for opening times ▪ Adm (free for EU members)

Almería, the "mirror of the sea", has lost much of its shine due to modern development. Still, its 10th-century Alcazaba is one of the most impressive surviving Moorish forts, and the engaging old quarter still seems North African in essence.

▶ **MORNING**

Begin your walk at **Plaza Bib-Rambla**, enhanced with flower stalls and the Neptune fountain. Fronting the western side of the square is the warren of ancient shopping streets called the **Alcaicería** *(see p120)*. Don't miss the 14th-century Moorish **Corral del Carbón**, which now houses a cultural centre.

Once the **cathedral** *(see pp116–17)* opens, it's time for a visit. Be sure to see the enormous Santiago el Matamoros (the Moorslayer) on horseback, by Alonso de Mena, adorning the altar of St James. The next stop is the **Capilla Real** *(see pp116–17)*; you should visit the crypt under the ostentatious marble sarcophagi of the kings and queens, where their bodies repose in plain lead boxes. On the carved Renaissance sepulchres, note the split pomegranate, symbol of a defeated Moorish Granada.

Continue on across the busy thoroughfares until you get to the river and the long expanse of **Plaza Nueva** *(see p59)*. Choose an outside table (the cafés here are all similar), order a drink and take in the street life.

It's time to enter the labyrinth of the **Albaicín** *(see pp16–17)*. Take **Calle Elvira** up to **Calle Calderería Vieja** for the vibrant bazaar of the Moorish Quarter. Following the old steep streets, keep going until you reach the fanciful **La Tetería del Bañuelo** *(see p122)*, an inviting place to sip some mint tea and sample Moroccan sweets.

*See map on pp116–17* ←

# Traditional Handicrafts

 **Albaicín, Granada**
The authentic Moroccan shops in this ancient quarter are all concentrated on two sloping streets off Calle Elvira – Calderería Vieja and Calderería Nueva (see pp16–17).

**2 Capricho del Artesano (Hermanos Fabres), Granada**
MAP Q2 ▪ Plaza Pescadería 10
▪ 958 28 81 92
This traditional ceramics store sells the typical style of the region: blue patterns on white tiles, often with a pomegranate motif.

**3 Taracea Laguna, Granada**
MAP S2 ▪ Real de la Alhambra 30 ▪ 958 22 70 46
Opposite the entrance to the Alhambra, you can see how taracea (Moorish marquetry, often inlaid with bone, mother of pearl or silver) is made, and take home a souvenir unique to this area.

 **Munira Mendonca, Granada**
MAP Q2 ▪ Plaza Nueva 15
▪ 958 22 19 39
Exquisitely hand-tooled leather goods, including bags and belts, can be found in this family-run shop.

 **El Rocío, Granada**
MAP Q2 ▪ C/Capuchinas 8
▪ 958 26 58 23
The complete outfitter for romería and festival-going gear. All the frills, polka dots and bright colours will dazzle your eye, and it all comes in every size, so even babies can have a flounce or two.

**6 Bazar el Valenciano, Almería**
MAP G4 ▪ C/Las Tiendas 34
▪ 950 23 45 93
This is the oldest store in town. Look for "El Indalo" souvenirs, items bearing the symbol of Almería for good luck.

**7 Hamza Soulimane, Granada**
MAP Q2 ▪ C/Ermita 10–13
▪ 958 22 53 45
A good array of all the traditional Moorish goods. Browse and bargain for tapestries and other handicrafts, tea sets, lamps, hookahs and more.

**8 La Alcaicería, Granada**
MAP Q2
In Moorish times this was the silk market, although the horseshoe arches and stucco are a modern re-creation. The narrow alleyways are bursting with colourful wares. Silver jewellery, embroidered silk shawls and ceramics are top buys.

**Narrow alleys of La Alcaicería**

**9 Alpujarras Crafts**
MAP F4–G4
The hill towns of this zone are rich in traditional crafts, including ceramics and weaving. Local jarapas (rugs), bags, ponchos and blankets are hand-loomed in age-old patterns. They're sold at local weekly markets.

**10 Níjar, Almería Province**
MAP H4
This coastal town is known for its distinctive pottery and jarapas. Head for Calle Las Eras, in the Barrio Alfarero, to find the genuine article.

# Nightlife

### ① El Camborio, Granada

MAP S1 ■ Camino del Sacromonte 47 ■ 958 22 12 15

This is a popular night venue in the caves of Sacromonte (see p17). Music echoes from four dance floors to the rooftop terraces, offering a striking view of the Alhambra at sunrise. The venue is open from Thursday to Saturday.

**Live flamenco show at Peña El Taranto**

### ② Granada 10, Granada

MAP Q2 ■ C/Carcél Baja 10 ■ 958 22 40 01

An opulent nightclub set in a 1930s theatre whose decor has been preserved. You can dance under crystal chandeliers, Neo-Classical-style plasterwork and plush private boxes. The music consists mainly of chart hits that attract people of all ages and styles.

### ③ San Matias 30, Granada

MAP Q2 ■ Plaza de las Descalzas 3 ■ 665 40 93 12

This trendy bar, located in the heart of Granada, is a popular spot with the locals. San Matias serves a variety of reasonably priced, delicious cocktails. The service is friendly and attentive.

### ④ Sala Prince, Granada

MAP R3 ■ Campo del Príncipe 7 ■ 625 62 29 06

This famous two-storey disco hosts live music by emerging artists as well as popular bands. The venue is styled after the Nasrid palaces on the hill above.

### ⑤ Planta Baja, Granada

MAP F4 ■ C/Horno de Abad 11 ■ 958 22 04 94

A two-storey venue: the upper floor is a quiet bar; downstairs, the DJs play chart hits and everyone dances. There is live music on weekends.

### ⑥ Peña El Taranto, Almería

MAP G4 ■ C/Tenor Iribarne 20 ■ 950 23 50 57

For lovers of real flamenco without tourist kitsch, this is the best place in the city (see p47).

### ⑦ Envidia, Granada

MAP F4 ■ C/Buensuceso 5 ■ 958 25 60 73

The vibe at this bar and club is gay-friendly, drawing a mixed crowd of locals and foreigners.

### ⑧ El Bribón de la Habana, Almería

MAP G5 ■ Puerto Deportivo de Aguadulce ■ 902 44 24 20

A three-level Cuban-themed club featuring Latin rhythms and the occasional cabaret show.

### ⑨ Maui Beach, Almería

MAP H4 ■ Paseo del Mediterráneo 40, Mojácar Beach ■ 950 47 87 22

This chiringuito (beach bar) has various zones, each with a great atmosphere. At night, it transforms from a bar-cum-restaurant into a lively club.

### ⑩ Le Chien Andalou, Granada

MAP R2 ■ Carrera del Darro 7 ■ 617 10 66 23

Dine while watching an enchanting flamenco show in a cosy cave setting. Reservations recommended.

*See map on pp116–17*

# Tearooms and Tapas Bars

### ① La Tetería del Bañuelo, Granada
**MAP R2 ■ C/Bañuelo 5**

A more relaxed and inviting place is hard to imagine. The little rooms and intimate niches are suffused with a gentle light, the air with the aromas of tea and flowers and the sound of songbirds. Try sweets and exotic brews, and enjoy unsurpassed views.

### ② Kasbah, Granada
**MAP Q2 ■ C/Calderería Nueva 4**

Relax amid the comforts of this candlelit café. Silky pillows and romantic nooks abound. You can taste Arab pastries and a selection of Moroccan teas.

**Casa Puga, a traditional tapas bar**

### ③ Casa Puga, Almería
**MAP G4 ■ C/Jovellanos 7**

One of the city's best tapas bars and reasonable, too. The wine list is exhaustive, as you might guess from the many wine racks on view.

### ④ Bar La Buena Vida, Granada
**MAP Q2 ■ C/Almiceros 12**

A welcoming tapas bar with a good variety of wines and beers. There's free tapas with each drink, so you can sample a wide variety of treats without breaking the bank.

### ⑤ La Riviera, Granada
**MAP Q2 ■ C/Cetti Meriem 7**

Located in the heart of the city, La Riviera offers a good variety of beer and tapas.

### ⑥ Antigua Bodega Castañeda, Granada
**MAP Q2 ■ C/Elvira 5**

Antique wine barrels and hanging hams give a rustic feel. The cheese boards are a good bet, as are the *montaditos* (small sandwiches).

### ⑦ Casa Enrique, Granada
**MAP Q3 ■ C/Acero de Darro 8**

Another wonderfully old-fashioned hole-in-the-wall lined with antique barrels. Try the *montaditos de lomo* (small sandwiches with pork fillet) and *torta del casar* (sheep's-milk cheese).

### ⑧ Tetería Al Hammam Almeraya, Almería
**MAP G4 ■ C/Perea 9**

Escape from the crowds of the town centre and head for the tranquil tea room of Almería's Arab baths, where you can enjoy Moorish-inspired teas and snacks. Opens at 4pm daily.

### ⑨ Bodega Francisco, Almuñécar
**MAP F5 ■ C/Real 15**

A forest of ham shanks hanging from the ceiling greets the eye, along with barrels of *fino* behind the bar in this traditional tapas bar. The attached restaurant next door, Francisco II, serves full meals.

### ⑩ El Quinto Toro, Almería
**MAP G4 ■ Juan Leal 6**

The name derives from the tradition that the best bull of a *corrida* is chosen to fight in the fifth (*quinto*) confrontation of the day. This tapas bar is favoured by local aficionados of the bullfight.

# Restaurants

### 1 Cunini, Granada

**MAP F4 ■ Plaza Pescadería 14 ■ 958 26 75 87 ■ Closed Sun D, Mon ■ €€**

The fresh seafood, brought in daily from Motril, is highly recommended, and is a big hit with the food critics.

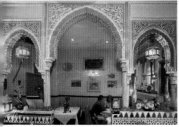

**Arrayanes Moroccan restaurant**

### 2 Arrayanes, Granada

**MAP Q2 ■ Cuesta Marañas 4 ■ 958 22 84 01 ■ Closed Tue ■ €**

A sophisticated and authentic North African restaurant in the Moroccan quarter. Halal meat and no alcohol.

### 3 Carmen Mirador de Aixa, Granada

**MAP R2 ■ Carril de San Agustín 2 ■ 958 22 36 16 ■ Closed Tue ■ €€**

The food is a taste of local culture with dishes such as *habas con jamón* (broad beans with ham). Views of the Alhambra from the terrace.

### 4 Restaurante El Ventorro, Alhama de Granada

**MAP E4 ■ Ctra de Jatar, km2 ■ 958 35 04 38 ■ Closed Mon ■ €€**

In this lovely rural restaurant you can try *choto al ajillo* (kid cooked with garlic) and other varieties of meat, as well as sumptuous *guisos* (stews).

### 5 Restaurante González, Trevélez

**MAP F4 ■ Plaza Francisco Abellán ■ 958 85 85 33 ■ €**

You are in a famous ham town so get what you came for – the dining room is hung with legs of meat.

**PRICE CATEGORIES**

For a three-course meal for one with half a bottle of wine (or equivalent meal), taxes and extra charges.

**€** under €30 **€€** €30–€50 **€€€** over €50

### 6 El Chaleco, Almuñécar

**MAP F5 ■ Avda Costa del Sol 37 ■ 958 63 24 02 ■ Closed Sun D, Mon (except Jul & Aug) ■ DA ■ €**

French cuisine, lovingly prepared with attention to detail, is served in a romantic, intimate setting.

### 7 La Tartana, La Herradura

**MAP F5 ■ La Tartana Hotel, Urbanización San Nicolas ■ 958 64 05 35 ■ €€**

This restaurant has a lovely terrace bar overlooking the sea. The menu changes seasonally and includes international fusion cuisine.

### 8 Pesetas, Salobreña

**MAP F5 ■ C/Bóveda 11 ■ 958 61 01 82 ■ €**

Absorb the ambience of the old quarters of Salobreña and the excellent views of the coast while dining here. The *choco a la marinera* (squid in tomato sauce) is a speciality. Good salads, too.

### 9 Restaurante Valentín, Almería

**MAP G4 ■ C/Tenor Iribarne 19 ■ 950 26 44 75 ■ Closed Mon, Sep ■ €€**

Specialities include *arroz negro* (rice in squid ink) and *pescado en adobo* (marinated fish).

### 10 La Goleta, San Miguel del Cabo de Gata

**MAP H5 ■ Paseo Marítimo Cabo de Gata ■ 950 37 02 15 ■ Closed Nov & Mon, Dec–May ■ €€**

All the seafood is at its freshest here, of course, since this village is located right in the middle of Andalucía's most unspoilt coast.

*See map on pp116–17*

# TOP 10 Córdoba and Jaén Provinces

These two provinces are an attractive blend of exquisite urban architecture, famed agricultural zones and great wildlife reserves within rugged mountain ranges. The ancient treasure-trove of Córdoba is the star, but the Renaissance towns of Baeza and Úbeda are among the region's most beautiful. For lovers of delicious wine, ham and olive oil, the areas around Montilla, Valle de los Pedroches and

**Iberian art, Museo Provincial de Jaén**

Baena should not be missed. Meanwhile, nature lovers can hike for days amid the wilds of the Parque Natural de la Sierra de Cardeña y Montoro in Córdoba and the Sierra de Cazorla in Jaén.

**Alcázar, Córdoba**

## 1 Córdoba

This town, wonderfully rich in history and cultural importance, is also small enough to cover easily and enjoyably on foot. It has a delightfully contrasting mix of sights, from the architectural splendour of the great mosque – with a Christian church oddly sprouting out of its centre – to the whitewashed glories of the old Jewish quarter, the splendid Alcázar and the Zoco Municipal with

**AREA MAP OF CÓRDOBA AND JAÉN PROVINCES**

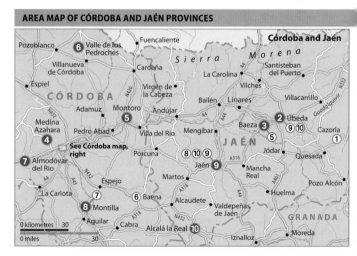

its diverse selection of goods made by local artists. There are engaging museums as well, featuring works of art by Old Masters and local artists, and ancient artifacts evoking the area's influential past *(see pp22–5)*.

## ② Úbeda

Ignore the downtrodden outskirts as you approach this town – once you get to the historic centre you will realize that it is one of Andalucía's most remarkable splendours. The keynote here is architecture – an entire district of Renaissance edifices built for local nobility in the 16th century. One of Andalucía's greatest architects, Andrés de Vandelvira, was the genius who gave most of these structures their harmonious forms *(see pp34–5)*.

## ③ Baeza

Like nearby Úbeda, this smaller town is also a jewel of Renaissance glory, but includes earlier remains dating back to the Moors and, before them, the Romans. The town radiates a sense of tranquillity as you walk from one cluster of lovely buildings to another. Again, much of the beauty owes its existence to the architect Andrés de Vandelvira *(see pp34–5)*.

Ruins of Medina Azahara palace

## ④ Medina Azahara

MAP D3 ■ Ctra Palma del Río km 5.5, W of Córdoba ■ 957 10 49 33 ■ Open Apr–mid-Jun: 9am–7:30pm Tue–Sat, 9am–3:30pm Sun & hols; mid-Jun–mid-Sep: 9am–3:30pm Tue–Sun & hols; mid-Sep–Mar: 9am–5:30pm Tue–Sat, 9am–3:30pm Sun & hols ■ Adm (free for EU members)

The building of the first palace here dates from AD 936, commissioned by Caliph Abd ar-Rahman III, Emir of Córdoba and the man who brought the city to glory. He named it after his favourite wife, Az-Zahra (the Radiant). Though it is little more than a ruin now, at one time it held a zoo, ponds and gardens, baths, houses, barracks, markets, mosques, a harem of 6,000 women and accommodation for 4,000 slaves.

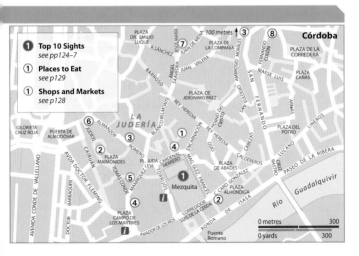

Top 10 Sights
see pp124–7

Places to Eat
see p129

Shops and Markets
see p128

### 5 Montoro

MAP E2 ■ Museo Arqueológico: Plaza de Santa María de la Mota; 957 16 00 89; open 11am–1pm Sat, Sun & pub hols ■ Casa de las Conchas: C/Criado 17; 957 49 16 77 (tourist office); adm

Laid out on an undulating series of five hills at a bend in the river, this ancient town sports a Baroque tower and a handsome 15th-century bridge. Other sights include a good Museo Arqueológico Municipal and the eccentrically kitsch Casa de las Conchas, a shell-encrusted folly; contact the tourist office for a tour.

### 6 Valle de los Pedroches

MAP D2

The far north of Córdoba Province is fertile grazing land for farm animals, as well as deer and wild boar. Most importantly, it is a "land of acorns", densely clad with holm oaks and therefore a prime zone for raising the famed Iberian black pig. In October, the creatures are fattened up on acorns and their meat is elaborately cured to produce succulent *jamón ibérico* or *pata negra*, the local product rivalling that of Jabugo in Huelva Province.

### 7 Castillo de Almodóvar

MAP D3 ■ Almodóvar del Río, 25 km (16 miles) W of Córdoba ■ 957 63 40 55 ■ Opening hours change monthly, check website for details ■ www.castillodealmodovar.com ■ Adm

Originally the site of a Roman, then a Moorish, fortification, the present fairy-tale castle goes back to the 1300s, when it was embellished in Gothic style. Legend holds that

**BAENA OLIVE OIL**

This Córdoba Province town is famed for its olive oil, and you can catch its unmistakable fragrance as you enter the district. The Museo del Olivar y el Aceite (C/Cañada 7 • 957 69 16 41 • Open Tue–Sun) is well worth a visit (above). It shows how each organically grown olive is carefully kept from bruising and the paste is extracted by the process of stone crushing.

ghosts of those who died while imprisoned here haunt the eight monolithic towers.

### 8 Montilla

MAP D3 ■ Bodegas Alvear: Avda de María Auxiliadora 1 ■ 957 65 01 00 ■ Open for tours in English 12:30pm Mon–Fri; by appt Sat, Sun & pub hols (groups of 7 or more) ■ Adm ■ www.alvear.es

The centre of Córdoba's wine-making region, this busy town gave *amontillado* sherry its name (it means "in the style of Montilla"). The wine produced here is like sherry, but nuttier and more toasted – and since the region is hotter than around Jerez, the grapes ripen more intensely and the wines need no fortifying. You can taste the difference at Bodegas Alvear, founded in 1729 *(see p76)*.

**Castillo de Almodóvar**

### 9 Jaén
MAP E3 ■ Cathedral: Plaza Santa María; open 10am–2pm & 4–8pm Mon–Fri, 10am–2pm & 4–7pm Sat, 10am–noon & 4–7pm Sun ■ Museo Provincial de Jaén: Paseo de la Estación 27; open Jun–mid-Sep: 9am–3:30pm Tue–Sat, 10am–5pm Sun; mid-Sep–May: 10am–8:30pm Tue–Sat, 10am–5pm Sun; adm (free for EU members)

This modern provincial capital is set off by the dramatically placed ramparts of the mighty Castillo de Santa Catalina (see p51) and the immensity of its double-towered cathedral by Vandelvira (see p53). You can experience the castle and its spectacular views of the city and surrounding olive groves, as it now houses a parador. The Museo Provincial de Jaén houses the country's finest collection of 5th-century BC Iberian sculpture.

**Castillo de Santa Catalina, Jaén**

### 10 Alcalá La Real
MAP E3 ■ Fortress: 639 64 77 96 ■ Open daily: Apr–mid-Oct 10:30am–7:30pm; mid-Oct–Mar: 10am–5:30pm (to 6pm Sat) ■ Adm

The Fortaleza de la Mota that dominates this once strategic town is unique in Jaén Province in that its original Moorish castle was built by the rulers of Granada. Mostly in ruins, it still preserves the original seven gates. Inside, built on the remains of a former mosque, is the Gothic-Mudéjar church of Santo Domingo, which uses the former minaret as a bell tower (see p50).

---

## A MORNING WALK THROUGH BAEZA

*[Map showing: Paseo de la Constitución, Torre de los Aliatares, Taberna El Pájara, La Alhóndiga, Fuente de los Leones, Plaza del Pópulo, Puerta de Jaén, Palacio de Jabalquinto, Plaza Santa María, Cathedral]*

### ▶ MORNING

Your tour of this Renaissance town starts at the lovely **Plaza del Pópulo** (see p34). The tourist office is inside a fine Plateresque palace, the Casa del Pópulo. Next to it are the arches of the **Puerta de Jaén** (see p34) and the Arco de Villalar, and in the centre is the **Fuente de los Leones**. The ruined lions and their eroded mistress, said to be a statue of Hannibal's wife, still manage to convey an undeniable elegance.

Exiting the square to the left of the tourist office, continue southeast to the **Plaza Santa María** (see p34) and the **cathedral**. Note the graffiti in bull's blood on the old seminary wall. Inside the cathedral, don't miss the extravagant choir screen by Bartolomé de Jaén.

Next stop, to the north, is the **Palacio de Jabalquinto** (see p34), with one of the most eccentric façades in the region, an example of Isabelline Plateresque style. It is now a university but you can still go in and visit its inner patio, then that of the Antigua Universidad next door.

Down the street, you can see the 1,000-year-old Moorish **Torre de los Aliatares** and around the corner, facing **Paseo de la Constitución** (see p34), **La Alhóndiga**, the old corn exchange, with its triple-tiered façade.

🍴 Have lunch at traditional **Taberna El Pájara**, with its rustic stone walls, local fare and extensive wine list *(Portales Tundidores 5 • 953 74 43 48 • Closed Mon • €€)*.

*See map on pp124–5* ←

# Shops and Markets

**Meryan leather workshop**

### (1) Meryan, Córdoba
MAP D3 ▪ Calleja de las Flores 2 ▪ 957 47 59 02

Specialists in hand-tooled leather goods; pick up a souvenir from your visit – from handbags, accessories and frames to furniture.

### (2) Zoco Municipal, Córdoba
MAP D3 ▪ C/Judios s/n ▪ 957 20 40 33

This historic house and patio has been converted into a co-op for local artists working in ceramics, leather, metalworks and woodwork.

### (3) Miró Arte en Plata, Córdoba
MAP D3 ▪ C/Claudio Marcelo 11 ▪ 615 82 78 35

Located just in front of the historic Templo Romano, this shop sells unique silver jewellery inspired by Córdoba's history and culture.

### (4) Bodegas Mezquita, Córdoba
MAP D3 ▪ C/Cardenal Herrero 8 ▪ 957 10 06 06

This is an excellent place for local foodstuffs: slow-cured hams, fine wines, olive oils and many other delectables. Their superb tapas bar is next door.

### (5) Baraka, Córdoba
MAP D3 ▪ C/Manriquez ▪ 957 48 83 27

For good-quality souvenirs this is a likely spot. Choose from ceramics, leather goods, glassware and other accessories, all handmade.

### (6) Nuñez de Prado, Baena
MAP E3 ▪ Avda de Cervantes 15 ▪ 957 67 01 41

One of the premier olive oil factories in this historic town (see p126). Their production methods have not compromised with modernity, so the oil remains rich and flavourful.

### (7) Monsieur Bourguignon, Córdoba
MAP D3 ▪ C/Jesús María 11 ▪ 605 98 75 84

A decadent shop offering an assortment of chocolates, biscuits and handmade sweets, which are almost too pretty to eat.

### (8) Galería de Vinos Caldos, Jaén
MAP E3 ▪ C/Ceron 12 ▪ 953 23 59 99

One of the area's best wine shops. It stocks regional wines, including those from Montilla (see p126).

### (9) Pottery Quarter, Úbeda
MAP F2 ▪ C/Valencia

Úbeda is famous for its dark green pottery, fired in wood kilns over olive stones. Its intricate, pierced designs are Moorish-inspired and the work-manship superb.

**Intricate green Úbeda pottery**

### (10) Flea Market, Jaén
MAP E3 ▪ Recinto Ferial, Avda de Granada

Thursday mornings see this street come to life with a catch-all market that can net you anything from pure junk to a rare treasure.

# Places to Eat

## 1 Restaurante & Bistró Casa Alfonso, Cazorla

MAP G3 ▪ Placeta Consuelo Mendieta 2 ▪ 953 72 14 63 ▪ Closed Tue ▪ DA ▪ €€

Expertly prepared dishes and attentive service in an elegant setting. Try one of the taster menus *(menu de degustación)*.

## 2 Horno San Luis, Córdoba

MAP D3 ▪ C/Cardenal Gonzalez 73 ▪ 665 05 37 83 ▪ €€

Housed in a historic *panaderia* (bread bakery), this stylish restaurant serves a varied cuisine.

## 3 El Churrasco, Córdoba

MAP D3 ▪ C/Romero 16 ▪ 957 29 08 19 ▪ Closed Aug ▪ €€€

One of the city's smartest eateries, serving traditional fare in a sumptuous setting. Sample the eponymous *churrasco* (grilled pork loin with spicy red pepper sauce).

## 4 Almudaina, Córdoba

MAP D3 ▪ Plaza Campo Santo de los Martires 1 ▪ 957 47 43 42 ▪ Closed Sun D ▪ €€

Set in a 16th-century mansion, this is another great place to try traditional dishes, such as *pechuga de perniz en salsa* (partridge breasts in sauce).

## 5 Xavi Taberna, Baeza

MAP F2 ▪ Portales Tundidores 8 ▪ 953 82 33 39 ▪ Closed Wed ▪ DA ▪ €€

An excellent choice of seafood, plus a number of vegetarian dishes, from the menu at this centrally located restaurant. There is also an extensive and reasonably priced wine list. The service is friendly and attentive.

## 6 Casa Rubio, Córdoba

MAP D3 ▪ Puerto Almodóvar 5 ▪ 957 42 08 53 ▪ Closed Wed ▪ €€

Built into the old city wall with Moorish arches and a stone floor, this atmospheric bar offers a good range of tapas.

## 7 Las Camachas, Montilla

MAP D3 ▪ Ctra Madrid-Málaga, Avda de Europa 3 ▪ 957 65 00 04 ▪ €€

Fish dishes are a speciality; go for the hake loin with clams and prawns, paired with the delightful local wine.

**The popular Taberna Salinas**

## 8 Taberna Salinas, Córdoba

MAP D3 ▪ C/Tundidores 3 ▪ 957 48 01 35 ▪ Closed Sun, Aug ▪ €

A bustling place, with dining rooms around a patio. Try the *naranjas picás con aceite y bacalao* (cod with orange and olive oil).

## 9 Taberna La Manchega, Jaén

MAP E3 ▪ C/Bernardo López 8 & Arco de Consuelo ▪ 953 23 21 92 ▪ Closed Tue, Aug ▪ €

An animated and authentic tapas bar. Downstairs they serve full meals, highlighting local meats.

## 10 Mesón Navarro, Úbeda

MAP F2 ▪ Plaza Ayuntamiento 2 ▪ 953 79 53 56 ▪ €

Something of a local institution. Try *pinchitos* (kebabs) and *ochios* (rolls).

*See map on pp124–5*

# Streetsmart

**Horse riders take part in the Feria
in Jerez de la Frontera**

# Getting To and Around Andalucía and the Costa del Sol

## Arriving by Air

Andalucía is served by airports in Málaga, Almería, Granada-Jaén, Jerez and Seville.

**Málaga–Costa del Sol Airport (AGP)** is Spain's fourth busiest, with frequent scheduled and charter connections to many European cities and seasonal services to Canada and the US. Regular buses run from the airport to Marbella (50 minutes, €9). Trains depart every 20 minutes on Line C1 for the **María Zabrano** station in Málaga, which is 14 km (8.6 miles) away; a one-way ticket costs €1.80 and the journey takes 8 minutes. In the opposite direction, the C1 stops at Torremolinos, Benalmádena and Fuengirola.

The much smaller **Almería (LEI)**, **Federico García Lorca Granada-Jaén (GRX)**, **Jerez de Frontera (XRY)** and **Seville (SVQ)** airports are served by domestic as well as European airlines, with chartered services increasing in the summer months. There are excellent public transport links from the airports to their nearest cities.

**Gibraltar (GIB)** airport operates flights to UK airports and to Morocco.

## Arriving by Rail

Spain's superfast **AVE** long-distance trains (see **Renfe** and **SNCF**) connect Madrid with Andalucía, departing from the capital's Puerta de Atocha station, stopping first at **Córdoba** (1 hour 40 minutes), before travelling onward to Málaga's **María Zambrano** station (in around 2 hours 20 minutes) or **Sevilla Santa Justa** (taking around 2 hours and 20 minutes).

There are also direct AVE trains from Barcelona Sants station to Seville, taking 5 hours and 25 minutes. A slower service connects Atocha Cercanías (the suburban terminal) in Madrid with Jaén (3 hours 45 minutes) and there are regular regional trains connecting these cities with Cádiz, Granada and Almería. As a guide, a one-way *turista* (second-class) ticket from Madrid to Málaga starts at €20.

Regional trains operate on the so-called Cercanías network across Andalucía. The Spanish rail operator, **Renfe**, sells a Spain Pass valid for 4, 6, 8, 10 and 12 journeys; as a guide, a 6-journey pass, to be used within one month, for an adult travelling in *turista* costs €234. Tickets and passes can be booked online in advance.

In July 2014, a light rail network, **Metro Málaga**, opened two of the planned six lines across the city of Málaga.

## Arriving by Bus

More than a dozen private bus companies operate across Andalucía and prices are often lower than the equivalent rail fares. There are frequent services between the main towns and cities and also day and overnight services to and from Madrid and Barcelona. As a guide, a direct bus from Cadiz to Granada with **ALSA** takes 5 hours and 15 minutes and costs €36.

Inside and around major cities, public transport is provided by multiple operators.

## Travelling by Car

With its sleepy rural villages, national and natural parks, dramatic mountain roads and excellent coastal highways, Andalucía lends itself to car hire. All airports have several providers and there are many more, often very competitive, smaller companies operating in the city centres. To hire a car you'll need a valid full driving licence, passport and credit card; some agencies will only accept customers over 21 or even 25 years.

The speed limit is 120 km/h (74 mph) on motor-ways/highways and dual carriageways, 100 km/h (62 mph) on roads with more than one lane in each direction and 90 km/h (55 mph) on all other ordinary roads, unless otherwise indicated. In urban areas, the speed can be as low as 20 km/h (12 mph).

Strict drink driving laws are in force. The general limit for drivers of private vehicles and cyclists is 0.05%. After a traffic accident, all those involved have to undergo a breath test. The **RAC** has further information for driving in Spain.

Parking can be very difficult, especially in the *pueblos blancos* where the roads are very narrow and there is limited parking availability; it is often best to park outside the old town areas and walk in.

## By Bicycle

Rural Andalucía is bicycle-friendly, with an extensive network of back roads, though steep inclines can be testing for inexperienced cyclists. For easier cycling, try the **Via Verde** – "Greenway" – established throughout Spain by converting unused railway lines into recreational areas for leisure cycling, walking and horse riding. There are routes through each province in Andalucía.

Bike hire is available in all the main towns and cities.

## By Taxi

All the towns and cities have taxi ranks, useful for short city hops but quite expensive for longer journeys – for example, the 60-km (37-mile) journey from Málaga to Marbella would cost in excess of €80.

For a more affordable option, visitors can use ridesharing services, such as **BlaBlaCar**, to travel between cities.

Málaga is famous for its Bike Taxis or Trixis. Passengers sit in a pod-like carriage, towed along behind a bicycle. You are completely covered, so it can be an all-weather travel option.

## On Foot

There are several long-distance trails

criss-crossing Andalucía. One of the most established is the **GR7**, which starts at Tarifa and runs through Málaga and Granada, connecting the region with northern Spain, Andorra and France before linking, in Alsace, to the E5 path. In Granada's wild interior, the GR7 hops from village to village. There is also run a (chargeable) luggage transfer service which will pick up or drop off bags from the start or end of your planned walk.

The Camino Mozárabe is a waymarked route which serves as a conduit for pilgrims from south-eastern Spain as it is part of the famous St James Way network (known as the Camino de Santiago). The Andalucian section runs for 396 km (246 miles) from Granada to Córdoba and then to Mérida where it picks up the route north to Santiago de Compostela.

## DIRECTORY

### AIRPORTS

**Málaga–Costa del Sol Airport**
( 91 321 10 00
w www.aena.es (which operates all Spain's main airports)

**Almería Airport**
( 91 321 10 00

**Federico García Lorca Granada-Jaén Airport**
( 91 321 10 00

**Jerez de la Frontera Airport**
( 91 321 10 00

**Seville**
( 91 321 10 00

### TRAINS

**Renfe**
( 902 320 320
w www.renfe.com

**Renfe Atendo service**
( 902 24 05 05

**SNCF**
w uk.voyages-sncf.com

**Estación Córdoba**
( 902 43 23 43

**Estación María Zambrano, Málaga**
( 902 43 23 43

**Estación Sevilla Santa Justa, Seville**
( 902 320 320

### LOCAL BUSES/METRO

**ALSA**
( 902 42 22 42 (24 hrs)
w www.alsa.es/en

**Avanza Grupo/Portillo**
( 902 450 550
w portillo.avanzabus.com

**Eurolines Málaga**
( 95 236 43 32
w www.eurolines.es

**Los Amarillos**
( 902 25 70 25
w samar.es

**Metro Málaga**
w metromalaga.es

### DRIVING

**RAC**
w www.rac.co.uk/driving-abroad/spain

### CYCLING/WALKING

**Via Verde**
w www.viasverdes.com

**GR7**
w www.gr7-granada.com

### TAXIS

**BlaBlaCar**
w www.blablacar.es

# Practical Information

## Passports and Visas

Visitors from outside the European Economic Area (EEA), European Union (EU) and Switzerland need a valid passport to enter Spain. EEA, EU and Swiss nationals can use identity cards instead.

Citizens of Canada, the US, Australia and New Zealand can visit Spain for up to 90 days without a visa as long as their passport is valid for 6 months beyond the date of entry. For longer stays, a visa is necessary. Most other non-EU nationals need a visa, and should consult the **Spanish Foreign Ministry** website or the Spanish Embassy in their country for details. Schengen visas are valid for Spain.

## Travel Safety Advice

Visitors can get up-to-date travel safety information from the **Foreign and Commonwealth Office** in the UK, the **US State Department** and the **Department of Foreign Affairs and Trade** in Australia.

## Customs and Immigration

For EU citizens there are no limits on most goods carried in or out of Spain as long as they are for personal use. Exceptions include firearms and weapons, some types of food and plants and endangered species.

Non-EU citizens may import 200 cigarettes and a litre of spirits per adult, and can get a refund on Spain's 21 per cent sales tax (VAT, known here as IVA) on purchases over €90.15 – do this at the airport when leaving.

## Health

Spain has an excellent public health service and the cities and coastal areas of Andalucía boast good hospitals and clinics. In an accident, or for urgent medical help, call the **emergency services** or the **Cruz Roja** (Red Cross), who will send an ambulance and paramedics. There are also dedicated lines for emergency dentists, narcotics or poisoning. If you are able to get to hospital, use the entrance marked Urgencias (Accident and Emergency). For less serious cases, visit one of the many private walk-in clinics. **Consulates** can provide a list of English-speaking physicians. Those covered by private health insurance can contact Doctors on Call.

No vaccinations are required to enter Spain, but routine vaccines should be kept up to date.

*Farmacias* (chemists or pharmacies), signalled by a green cross or a white cross on a green background, can offer advice for medical treat-ment. After hours, the nearest all-night pharmacy is posted on the door of each outlet, or call **Pharmacy on Duty** (or look online for Farmácias de Guardia) to locate the nearest.

Emergency contraception is available on prescription.

Visitors who suspect they may have caught a sexually transmitted disease (STD) can have on-the-spot tests done at most hospitals.

## Insurance

All travellers are advised to buy insurance against accidents, illness, theft or loss and travel delays or cancellations. Spain has a reciprocal health agreement with other EU countries, and EU citizens receive emergency treatment under the public healthcare system if carrying a valid European Health Insurance Card (EHIC). Prescriptions have to be paid for up-front. Non-EU visitors should check (with their embassy) to see if there are reciprocal arrangements with Spain.

## Personal Security

Spain is generally safe, but care should be taken in crowded trains, stations and busy tourist areas where pickpockets tend to operate. Some of the marginal areas in the main cities have seen gang violence and while this is usually limited to local disputes, such areas should be avoided especially after dark.

Try not to carry any valuables in easily visible or accessible places, or use a money belt. Never leave bags unattended.

If you lose belongings, all major airports and railway stations have lost property *(objetos perdidos)* offices. If the item has not been found you will be asked to complete a Formulario de Reclamación de Objetos Perdidos.

Spain is generally safe for women travelling alone, but stick to busy areas after dark, avoid empty train carriages, and sit near the driver's compartment on buses.

## Disabled Travellers

Visitors with mobility issues will find coastal areas are reasonably well-equipped for their needs. Pavements in urban areas are sloped at junctions for the benefit of wheelchair users. Most public buildings, shopping malls and cinemas are fitted with lifts, ramps and extra-wide doors. **Blue Badge Mobility** rents out wheelchairs and scooters for visitors to the Costa del Sol.

Most trains are wheelchair accessible and **Renfe**, Spain's national rail operator, has a 24-hour service, **Atendo**, for passengers with disabilities on high speed and ordinary trains. When calling, passengers must advise if they are travelling in their own wheelchair and need an H-seat, in a folding wheelchair travelling in a regular seat, have an auditory or visual disability but without a guide dog/attendant, or have reduced mobility.

All buses displaying a wheelchair symbol are equipped for disabled access; many buses in cities and towns have one door with a ramp that can be lowered.

## DIRECTORY

### PASSPORTS AND VISAS

**Spanish Foreign Ministry**
w exteriores.gob.es

### CONSULATES

**Canada**
Plaza de la Malagueta 2, Málaga
c 952 22 33 46

**Ireland (Hon consul)**
Galerías Santa Monica, Avenida Los Boliches 15, Fuengirola
c 952 47 51 08

**UK**
C/Mauricio Moro Pareto 2, Edificio Eurocom, Málaga
c 952 35 92 11

**USA**
Avenida Juan Gómez, 8 Edificio Lucía, Fuengirola
c 952 47 48 91

### TRAVEL SAFETY ADVICE

**Australian Department of Foreign Affairs and Trade**
w dfat.gov.au
w smartraveller.gov.au

**UK Foreign and Commonwealth Office**
w gov.uk/foreign-travel-advice

**US State Department**
w travel.state.gov

### EMERGENCY SERVICES

**Ambulance**
c 061 or 112

**Cruz Roja (Red Cross)**
c 952 44 35 45

**Fire**
c 080 or 112

**Police**
c 091 or 112

**Municipal Police**
c 092

**Emergency – Dentist**
c 961 49 61 99

**Emergency – Narcotics**
c 915 62 05 20

**Emergency – Poison**
c 915 62 04 20

### HEALTH SERVICES

**Doctors on Call**
c 112

**HIV/Aids**
c 902 42 44 24

**Hospital Costa del Sol**
Ctra Nacional Autovía A7, Marbella
c 951 97 66 69

**Hospital Reina Sofía, Córdoba**
Avda Menéndez Pidal
c 957 01 00 00

**Hospital Victoria Eugenia, Seville**
Avda de la Cruz Roja, 1
c 954 35 14 00

**Hospital Virgen de las Nieves, Granada**
Avda de las Fuerzas Armadas 2
c 958 02 00 00

**Pharmacy on Duty**
c 963 60 03 13

### DISABLED TRAVELLERS

**Blue Badge Mobility**
c 952 96 70 15
w bluebadgemobility.com

**Atendo**
c 902 24 05 05 (24 hrs)

## Currency and Banking

Spain is one of the 19 European countries using the euro (€). It is divided into 100 cents, with paper notes in denominations of €5, €10, €20, €50, €100, €200 and €500. Coins are €2, €1, 50c, 20c, 10c, 5c, 2c and 1c.

You will be able to buy euros at local branches of banks in Spain and also at *casas de cambio* (bureaux de change); many of the latter can be found at train stations.

Cash machines or ATMs *(cajeros automáticos)* are dotted throughout cities and towns. Expect to pay a handling fee if you withdraw cash from a bank not affiliated with your own. Stiff fees are charged by "independent" ATMs. Ask about credit card ATM cash withdrawal fees (which can be high) before you go.

**Mastercard** and **VISA** credit and debit cards are accepted by many cafés, restaurants and shops but not all, so it is wise to carry some cash. **Diners Club** and **American Express** are less useful.

Should any of your cards be lost/stolen, it is essential to inform your bank immediately.

Prepaid currency cards (cash passports) can be pre-loaded with euros, fixing exchange rates before you leave, and used like a debit card.

Traveller's cheques can be exchanged at all larger banks or at branches of the issuers. Most banks charge a fee. Hotels will also change money but may charge higher fees.

## Internet and Telephone

Spaniards are more wired than ever. Cities and towns across Andalucía are provided with plenty of wireless Internet hotspots – many of them free – in bars, cafés, department stores, hotels and some public spaces.

It is advisable to sign up for an international usage plan for your phone to keep costs down. Or, on arrival, consider buying a local SIM card or cheap mobile phone with a Spanish number so you can take advantage of local rates. If needed, ask your home carrier for the unlock code to use a different SIM card/service.

There are public phones (both enclosed booths and open handsets) in town and city centres, though they are slowly vanishing. Most are card-operated, but a few will take coins. Phone cards can be bought from post offices, department stores and kiosks.

## Time Difference

Spain is on Central European Time (CET), an hour ahead of Greenwich Mean Time, 6 hours ahead of US Eastern Standard Time and 11 hours behind Australian Eastern Standard Time. The clock moves forward 1 hour during daylight saving time from the last Sunday in March until the last Sunday in October.

## Postal Services

Spanish mail is efficient, reliable and fast. There are around 10,000 offices of *Correos*, the national mail service; opening hours vary widely, with many rural offices only open in the mornings.

Buy stamps from the post office or vending machines (often outside the entrance). A standard letter weighing up to 20 g or a postcard to anywhere outside Spain costs €0.40.

## TV, Radio and Newspapers

Televisión Española (TVE), the state-owned national network, operates five main channels, including a sports channel, 24-hour news and children's programmes – *Clan*. Private channels, such as Telecinco and Antena 3, have stolen a big chunk of their audience. Thanks to satellite and cable you can watch global English channels including BBC World and CNN.

The state-owned Radio Nacional de España (RNE) operates six stations, including Radio Clásica, which plays mainly classical music, and Radio 5, a 24-hour news service. There are private channels in all regions. Global Radio (93.6 MHz) and Spectrum FM (several frequencies) broadcast in English across the Costa del Sol.

National newspapers include *El País*, *El Mundo*, and *ABC Sur*. Based in Málaga, the latter is the best-selling daily newspaper in Andalucía and produces an English-language edition. The *Olive Press* is a web-based English-language news source. *Costa Link* is a free local magazine with cinema and event listings.

## Electrical Appliances

The electric current is 220 volts. Many electrical appliances such as hair dryers have 110/220 V transformers built in, so converters may be less of a concern, especially if you're coming from North America. Some hotel bathrooms use a lower current as a safety measure. Plug sockets are Type C, as is common throughout mainland Europe, so bring adaptors with two round pins.

## Weather

The mild, Mediterranean climate in Andalucía is the envy of much of Europe. The year-round average temperature is 18–20° C (64–68° F) with 320 sunny days. Coastal areas have highs fluctuating between 15° C (59° F) and 30° C (86° F). Inland, average city highs vary from 12° C (54° F) in January to an uncomfortable 36° C (97° F) in August.

Along the Costa del Sol it is mild and dry from April to September, very hot in July and August, and cool and wet in winter. Inland the temperature climbs where the wind is absent and falls where the land rises signifi-cantly, as in the Sierra Nevada and Alpujarra. Nights can be cool even in high summer.

Every season offers its reasons to come here: summer for nightlife, spring and autumn for nature, winter for skiing. But autumn is arguably the best time – the weather and water are still warm, the crowds have gone, prices are lower and there are lots of local festivals.

## Visitor Information

There are official **tourist information** booths at the airport and in cities and bigger towns; opening times vary widely but all operate in the mornings even during low season.

Here you can get maps and city passes that allow discounts on sights and local travel, or arrange city tours or hop on/hop off bus tours. Tourist information booths are immensely useful for finding out what's on locally, from *fiestas* and flamenco to operas or gay venues, and will often book tickets for cultural events for you.

## Gay, Lesbian and Transgender Travellers

In more cosmopolitan areas, attitudes towards gays and lesbians are relaxed, but less so in rural areas. Torremolinos is a major centre for gay nightlife *(see p110)*. Seville, Granada and Cádiz also have thriving gay popu-lations. Find out more from the **International Gay & Lesbian Travel Association** and the local **Federación Colegas**, which has centres in Córdoba, Seville, Málaga and Almería.

---

## DIRECTORY

### POSTAL SERVICES
w correos.es
c 902 19 71 97

### VISITOR INFORMATION

**Alcazaba Information**
Plaza Aduana, Málaga

**Andalucía**
w andalucía.org
w spain.info

**Consorcio de Turismo de Córdoba**
C/Rey Heredia 22, Córdoba
c 957 20 17 74
w english.turismode cordoba.org

**Federación Colegas**
c 954 50 13 77
w andalucía.colegaweb.org

**Granada**
w granada.org

**Granada Municipal Tourist Office**
Ayuntamiento de Granada, Plaza del Carmen
c 958 24 82 80
w granadatur.com

**International Gay and Lesbian Travel Association**
w iglta.org

**Málaga Airport**
MAP E5 ▪ Terminal 3
c 951 29 40 03

**Málaga Municipal Tourism Central Office**
Plaza de la Marina
c 951 92 60 20

**Oficina Sevilla Centro**
Plaza San Francisco 19, Seville (next to the Town Hall)
c 955 47 12 32
w visitasevilla.es

**Seville Airport**
Avda Autopista de San Pablo
c 954 78 20 35

**Sevilla Santa Justa Train Station**
Avda Kansas City
c 954 78 20 02

## Specialist Tours

Hiking, horse riding and cycling are ideal ways to explore the Andalucian countryside, and many companies offer group trips. You can book before coming or through a local organization, such as **Federación Española de Deportes de Montaña** or **Nevadensis**. Self-guided walking holidays with bag transfer is also an option.

Nature lovers can look out for birds, or watch whales or dolphins at the Straits of Gibraltar (try **Turmares Tarifa**, or the Gibraltar-based **Dolphin Safari**). Or go on a safari with **Safari del Sol**.

Tours of the *bodegas* (wine cellars) are a must if you are in the "Sherry Triangle" or Málaga, with samplings of wines as well as gastronomic delights *(see pp76–7)*. Try **Saranjan Tours** or **Wine Tours of Spain**.

Get a feel for more of the flavours of Andalucía by learning to cook regional dishes or dance the flamenco-based Sevillana (established operators include **Taller Flamenco** in Seville).

Combining a holiday with Spanish lessons is a popular choice. The **Instituto Cervantes** is an official organization set up to promote Spanish. Or try the **Center for Cross-Cultural Study** in Seville, and Málaga's **Instituto de Español Picasso**.

Many companies organize art, architecture, archaeology and music-themed tours. Local specialists include **Paint Andalucía** on the Costa del Sol, and **Los Gázquez** in Almería, who arrange photography trails. A useful search engine to get started is **Responsible Travel**, which gathers ideas from tour operators.

View Andalucía from the sea while sailing at one of the many water sports clubs along the coast. Or learn to kitesurf on the wild Costa de la Luz; schools include **Tarifa Max Kitesurf School** *(see pp66)*.

Or take a tour of the greens: with more than 50 golf courses on the Costa del Sol *(see p109)* there are many specialist operators.

**Glovento Sur** offers balloon flights over Granada, Ronda and other beautiful spots.

## Shopping

As in any region that is very popular with international tourists, there can be a lot of tat on sale – from hand-held plastic fans to maracas and slogan T-shirts, none of which are made here. But quality locally made goods are available. In Seville, for instance, there are beautiful hand-crafted guitars for sale as well as authentic flamenco dresses and shoes.

For big brands, the cities and Marbella boast big shopping centres and, in the latter, glitzy high streets. Most of the top-end brands can be found in Puerto Banús and in the centre of Marbella on Avenida Ricardo Soriano.

## Opening Hours

Typical business hours are Monday–Saturday, from 9:30am–1:30pm, and 4:30 to 8pm. Major shopping centres and department stores are open all day from 10am–9pm. Main stores and shopping centres also open their doors to the public on some Sundays in the year. In the high season in coastal areas many stay open until after 10pm. Big supermarkets are open 9am–10pm. Smaller stores usually close by 3pm on Saturday.

## Dining

Eating out is one of the high points of a holiday in Andalucía. Recognized centres of gastronomy include Málaga, Marbella, Ronda, Granada and Seville, but there are wonderful restaurants in out-of-the-way places. Fish and seafood are excellent on the coast, but even in Córdoba it is easy to get fresh squid and the morning's hake. Pork in all its guises is the central meat in the Andalucian diet. Vegetarian and vegan options are still few and far between and vegetable dishes are often enhanced with a bit of pork. Most chefs will make a salad, leaving out any non-vegetarian ingredients and there are usually vegetable tapas.

The regional drink of choice is *vino de Jerez* (sherry), or one of the sweet wines from Málaga, though Tinto de Verano (red wine spritzer) is prevalent, too.

Choose the cheaper *menú del día* (daily menu) at lunch. You get a limited choice of a first course (typically soup or salad) and second course and dessert, with bread and a beverage included.

Although tipping is not an absolute necessity, it is customary to leave about 5 per cent of the total bill.

People eat late in this part of Spain. Lunchtime is rarely before 2pm. Dinner is no earlier than 9pm and dining as late as 11pm is not unheard of, particularly in the summer. Visitors should note that restaurants are usually closed on Mondays.

## Where to Stay

Whatever your budget, finding a good, affordable place to stay in Andalucía generally isn't a problem. It is not hard to find double rooms in great locations for between €50

and €100. A popular tourist destination, there is a glut of beds, especially in coastal resorts, and conversions of old buildings has led to a boom in small, boutique-style hotels, especially in cities. **Paradores de Turismo de España** – usually shortened to Paradores – is a large state-run chain of Spanish luxury hotels who, since 1928, have converted many character properties, often former convents, ducal mansions and castles, into hotels. Sites such as **Laterooms**, **Booking.com** and **Trivago** can help you explore the range of options, while **Airbnb** and similar are good places to look for

private villas, rooms and apartments. Youth hostels here are generally well equipped and suitable for all ages.

Most accommodation options – unless they specifically request "adults only" – truly welcome families. Hotels often allow you to include children up to a certain age – sometimes as high as teens – at no extra charge, except perhaps a nominal fee for the extra bed or two. Many resorts and clubs include free entertainment and activities for children, and often for teens, although the best option for families may be a self-catering property.

## DIRECTORY

### SPECIALIST TOURS

**Air Born Adventures**
670 43 11 65
airbornadventures.com

**Center for Cross-Cultural Study in Seville**
954 22 41 07
cccs.com

**Club de Mar de Almería (sailing)**
950 23 07 80
clubdemaralmeria.es

**Dolphin Safari**
dolphinsafari.gi

**Federación Española de Deportes de Montaña**
958 29 13 40
fedamon.com

**Glovento Sur**
958 29 03 16
gloventosur.com

**Instituto Cervantes**
londres.cervantes.es
nyork.cervantes.es

**Instituto de Español Picasso in Málaga**
952 21 39 32
insituto-picasso.com

**Los Caballos de Mosquin**
608 65 81 08
horseridingandalucia.com

**Los Gázquez**
losgazquez.com

**Nevadensis**
Pampaneira, Granada
958 76 31 27
nevadensis.com

**Paint Andalucía on the Costa del Sol**
618 23 43 67
paint-andalucia.com

**Real Club Mediterraneo (sailing)**
952 22 63 00
realclubmediterraneo.com

**Responsible Travel**
responsibletravel.com

**Safari del Sol**
Benahavis, Málaga
633 50 64 66
safaridelsol.com

**Saranjan Tours**
800 858 95 94
saranjan.com

**Taller Flamenco in Seville**
954 56 42 34
tallerflamenco.com

**Tarifa Max Kitesurf School**
696 55 82 27
kiteschooltarifa.net

**Turmares Tarifa**
turmares.com

**Wine Tours of Spain**
911 43 65 53
cellartours.com

### WHERE TO STAY

**Airbnb**
airbnb.com

**Booking.com**
booking.com

**Laterooms**
laterooms.com

**Paradores de Turismo de España**
parador.es/en

**Trivago**
trivago.com

# Places to Stay

**PRICE CATEGORIES**
For a standard, double room per night (with breakfast if included), taxes and extra charges.

€ under €100    €€ €100–€200    €€€ over €200

## Seville Stays

### Hotel Un Patio al Sur
MAP L2 ▪ C/Fernán Caballero 7 ▪ 954 22 10 35 ▪ www.patioalsur.es ▪ Disabled access ▪ €
Housed in an 18th-century Andalucian mansion, this hotel is conveniently located near the Museo de Bellas Artes. The rooftop terrace offers wonderful city views. Free Wi-Fi.

### Oasis Backpackers' Palace
MAP L2 ▪ C/Almirante Ulloa 1 ▪ 955 26 26 96 ▪ www.oasisseville.com ▪ €
Once a grand palace, this hostel has spacious dorms and double rooms with en-suite bathrooms. There's free Wi-Fi, a shared kitchen, lounge, and rooftop pool.

### Alcoba del Rey
MAP N1 ▪ C/Becquer 9 ▪ 954 91 58 00 ▪ www.alcobadelrey.com ▪ Disabled access ▪ €€
Boutique hotel with Indian- and Moroccan- style decor and king-size canopy beds. Great views from the rooftop terrace. Free Wi-Fi.

### H10 Corregidor Boutique Hotel
MAP M1 ▪ C/Morgado 17 ▪ 954 38 51 11 ▪ www.h10hotels.com ▪ €€
Just around the corner from the lively Alameda de Hercules, in a bohemian part of town, this hotel is clean and comfortable. It also provides free access to a gym across the street. Free Wi-Fi.

### Hotel Taberna del Alabardero
MAP L3 ▪ C/Zaragoza 20 ▪ 954 50 27 21 ▪ www.tabernadelalabardero.es ▪ Disabled access ▪ €€
Seven elegant rooms are gathered around a central patio filled with greenery. There is also a spa and a Michelin-starred restaurant. Free Wi-Fi.

### Murillo Apartamentos
MAP M4 ▪ Lope de Rueda 16 ▪ 954 21 60 95 ▪ www.hotelmurillo.com ▪ Disabled access ▪ €€
These lovely apartments are named after the Baroque painter who hailed from the flower-decked old quarter, where they are located. Free Wi-Fi.

### Las Casas del Rey de Baeza
MAP N2 ▪ Plaza Jesús de la Redención 2 ▪ 954 56 14 96 ▪ www.hospes.es ▪ Disabled access ▪ €€€
Close to La Casa de Pilatos, this chic hotel is located in a beautiful setting, which fuses historic traditional architecture with modern style. Shaded walkways and stone flooring echo the natural tones in the courtyards. The rooftop pool is a bonus.

### EME Catedral Hotel
MAP M3 ▪ C/Alemanes 27 ▪ 954 56 00 00 ▪ www.emecatedralhotel.com ▪ Disabled access ▪ €€€
Opposite the cathedral, this hotel has a trendy ambience. Highlights include a spa, an excellent Italian eatery, a Mediterranean-fusion bistro and a rooftop lounge with unparalleled views.

### Eurostars Sevilla Boutique
MAP M2 ▪ C/Abades 41 ▪ 954 97 90 09 ▪ www.eurostarshotels.co.uk ▪ Disabled access ▪ €€€
In the heart of Barrio de Santa Cruz, with excellent views of the Giralda and the cathedral from its roof terrace, expect minimalist luxury in contrast to the classic façade. There's an outdoor pool.

### Hotel Alfonso XIII
MAP M4 ▪ C/San Fernando 2 ▪ 954 91 70 00 ▪ www.hotel-alfonsoxiii-seville.com ▪ Disabled access ▪ €€€
This historic palace, now a five-star hotel, was erected by the eponymous king to house royals and other dignitaries during the 1929 Exposition. Rooms are luxuriously decorated, and the hotel has an outdoor swimming pool with alfresco dining alongside.

### Meliá Colón Hotel
MAP L2 ▪ C/Canalejas 1 ▪ 954 50 55 99 ▪ www.solmelia.com ▪ Disabled access ▪ €€€
This grand five-star hotel combines Andalucian elegance and maximum comfort. Enjoy fabulous

views from the solarium, cool off in the pool or relax in the spa. The cocktail bar hosts live music.

## Granada Stays

### Cuevas El Abanico
MAP F4 ▪ Verea de Enmedio ▪ 958 22 61 99 ▪ www. cuevaselabanico.es ▪ €
The whitewashed interior of this self-catering "cave" hotel is immaculate and loaded with rustic charm. No need for air conditioning – you have an entire hill of earth overhead to keep out the heat. Picturesque and uniquely Andalucian. Minimum two-night stay.

### Hotel Zawan del Darro
MAP R2 ▪ Carrera del Darro 23 ▪ 958 21 57 30 ▪ www.hotelzawan deldarro.com ▪ Disabled access ▪ €
A former Franciscan convent, this 16th-century palace has been restored in its original style. Some of the rooms have spectacular views. Free Wi-Fi.

### Oasis Backpackers' Hostel
MAP Q2 ▪ Placeta Correo Viejo 3 ▪ 958 21 58 48 ▪ www.oasisgranada. com/granada-hostel ▪ €
Set in a historic building, this hostel has a rooftop terrace with great views, an interior patio, a bar, a kitchen and free Wi-Fi. Most rooms are en-suite.

### Pension Suecia
MAP R3 ▪ C/Molinos (Huerta de los Angeles) 8 ▪ 958 22 50 44 ▪ www. pensionsuecia.com ▪ €
In a leafy cul-de-sac, this traditional Andalucian house has arched windows, terracotta tiles

and a patio. The rooftop terrace is perfect for admiring the nearby Alhambra. Free Wi-Fi.

### Posada Pilar del Toro
MAP Q2 ▪ C/Elvira 25 ▪ 958 22 73 33 ▪ www. posadadeltoro.com ▪ Disabled access ▪ €
In the heart of the Albaicín, this *posada* features traditional wooden beams and ceramic tiles, creating a rustic ambience with modern comforts.

### Santa Ana Apartamentos Turísticos, Granada
MAP F4 ▪ Puente Cabrera 9 ▪ 671 03 74 00 ▪ www. santaanaapartamento. com ▪ €
Situated just above the river, these apartments come with views of the Albaicín quarter. Each apartment has large, stylish rooms. Minimum two-night stay. Free Wi-Fi.

### Hotel Reina Cristina
MAP F4 ▪ C/Tablas 4 ▪ 958 25 32 11 ▪ www. hotelreinacristina.com ▪ €€
Everything has been kept more or less the same as when the poet García Lorca was forced to hide out here – this is the last place the poet stayed, before his untimely end *(see p49)*. Each room has a unique style and there are patios and fountains in the public areas.

### El Ladrón de Agua
MAP R2 ▪ Carrera del Darro 13 ▪ 958 21 50 40 ▪ www.ladrondeagua. com ▪ €€
This superbly located boutique hotel is set in a 16th-century mansion. Eight of the beautifully

decorated rooms have views of the Alhambra. Guests can enjoy complimentary appetizers and regional wines every evening.

### Alhambra Palace
MAP R3 ▪ Plaza Arquitecto García de Paredes 1 ▪ 958 22 14 68 ▪ www.h-alhambra palace.es ▪ Disabled access ▪ €€€
The style of this *belle époque* extravaganza is Neo-Moorish. The public rooms are palatial. Just steps away from the Nasrid palace, it has great views from every room, terrace and balcony.

### Room Mate Leo
MAP Q3 ▪ C/Mesones 15 ▪ 958 53 55 79 ▪ www. room-matehotels.com ▪ Disabled access ▪ €€€
This trendy hotel is located on a pedestrianised street within walking distance of most sights. There are stunning views of the Alhambra and the city from the top floor terrace and some rooms, which are modern, with a creative mix of colour and decor. There's a breakfast buffet available until noon.

## Paradors

### Parador Alcázar del Rey, Carmona
MAP C3 ▪ Alcázar s/n ▪ 954 14 10 10 ▪ €€
One of the most impressive of all the paradors, this 14th-century Moorish fortress-palace overlooks the Río Corbones. Rooms are large and decorated in classic Andalucian style, set off by antiques. Cool off in the garden pool or on the expansive terrace.

### Parador de Antequera

MAP D4 ▪ Paseo García del Olmo 2 ▪ 952 84 02 61 ▪ Disabled access ▪ €€
This quiet parador, surrounded by gardens and a swimming pool, is near the spectacular El Torcal (see p61).

### Parador Arcos de la Frontera

MAP C5 ▪ Plaza del Cabildo ▪ 956 70 05 00 ▪ Disabled access ▪ €€
Right on the banks of the Río Guadalete, this has an impressive view of the fertile plain of the river and of the old part of town. An ideal starting point for the pueblos blancos routes, as well as Jerez de la Frontera. The courtyard is graced with traditional latticework and ceramic tiles.

### Parador de Ayamonte

MAP A4 ▪ Avda de la Constitucíon ▪ 959 32 07 00 ▪ Disabled access ▪ €€
A modern facility with sunlit rooms and a perfect position for exploring the area where Huelva Province meets Portugal. Most rooms afford panoramic views of the Atlantic from the high point of town.

### Parador de Cazorla

MAP G3 ▪ 953 72 70 75 ▪ Sierra de Cazorla s/n ▪ Closed mid-Dec–Feb ▪ €€
In a remote location in the heart of the Parque Natural Sierra de Cazorla, with stunning views, this graceful country house lets you get away from it all in comfort. The restaurant offers regional fare and game in season.

### Parador Condestable Dávalos, Úbeda

MAP F2 ▪ Plaza de Vázquez Molina ▪ 953 75 03 45 ▪ €€
Live like 16th-century nobility in a Renaissance palace in the heart of one of Spain's best preserved historic centres. Rooms reflect the noble tone, with high ceilings and antique furnishings.

### Parador de Mójacar

MAP H4 ▪ Paseo del Mediterraneo 339 ▪ 950 47 82 50 ▪ Disabled access ▪ €€
This beachside parador, 1.5 km (1 mile) from the village of Mójacar and 3 km (just under 2 miles) from a golf course, has an inviting atmosphere with spectacular views from the bedroom terraces and the upstairs dining room. Ultra-modern, clean and child-friendly.

### Parador del Gilbralfaro, Málaga

MAP S4 ▪ Castillo de Gibralfaro ▪ 952 22 19 02 ▪ Disabled access ▪ €€€
This parador stands surrounded by pine trees, facing the Alcázaba. It's handy for golf courses and tennis nearby.

### Parador de Mazagón

MAP B4 ▪ Playa de Mazagón ▪ 959 53 63 00 ▪ Disabled access ▪ €€€
Unspoiled beauty on the shores of the sea is what this modern property is all about. It's ideal for those who want to commune with nature, especially with the wonders of the Coto Doñana, nearby. Facilities include gardens, pools and a sauna – all facing Mazagón beach.

### Parador de Ronda

MAP D5 ▪ Plaza de España ▪ 952 87 75 00 ▪ Disabled access ▪ €€€
Set in the former town hall; views from the rooms are amazing, while the decor reflects the colours of the area.

### Parador de San Francisco, Granada

MAP S3 ▪ C/Real de la Alhambra ▪ 958 22 14 40 ▪ €€€
You'll need to book about a year in advance to lodge here, but it's the premier stay in town. Housed in a meticulously restored 15th-century monastery, with a wisteria-covered patio, it is truly beautiful. For the maximum experience, get a room with a view out over the Albaicín on one side and the cloister on the other.

## Luxury Hotels

### Casa Vesta, Zufre

MAP B3 ▪ C/Santa Zita, Zufre ▪ 959 19 80 96 ▪ www.casa-vesta.com ▪ Disabled access ▪ €€
Located in the countryside of Huelva, this charming boutique hotel has world-class service and boasts a billiards room, library, outdoor swimming pool and free Wi-Fi. No under-16s.

### Club Marítimo de Sotogrande

MAP C6 ▪ Puerto Deportivo, Sotogrande ▪ 956 79 02 00 ▪ www.slh.com/maritimo ▪ Disabled access ▪ €€
Luxurious and tastefully decorated in neutral tones, this hotel affords amazing views from every room – sometimes from the bathtub. Free bike use and discounts for golfing.

### Hotel Montelirio, Ronda

MAP D5 ▪ C/Tenorio 8
▪ 952 87 38 55 ▪ www.
hotelmontelirio.com
▪ Disabled access ▪ €€
A beautifully restored
17th-century palace
offering every comfort.
Perched on the edge of
Ronda's famous gorge,
it has stunning views.
There's an outdoor pool
and a Turkish bath.

### Husa Palacio de Mengibar

MAP E2 ▪ Plaza
Constitución 8, Mengibar
▪ 953 37 40 43 ▪ www.
palaciodemengibar.com
▪ Disabled access ▪ €€
This artistically restored
stately palace serves
haute cuisine in the rustic
restaurant housed in the
old stables. Rooms are
individually decorated and
there is a lovely courtyard.

### El Fuerte, Marbella

MAP D5 ▪ Avda El Fuerte
▪ 952 86 15 00 ▪ www.
fuertehoteles.com
▪ Disabled access ▪ €€€
In the centre of Marbella,
next to the sea and
surrounded by subtropical
gardens. Within easy
walking distance of the
historic quarter too, so
you can discover the
"real" Marbella, as well
as soak up the glamour.

### Hospes Palacio del Baílio, Córdoba

MAP D3 ▪ Ramírez de las
Casas Deza 10–12 ▪ 957
49 89 93 ▪ www.hospes.
es ▪ Disabled access
▪ €€€
Dating back to the 16th
century, this hotel is a complex of former granaries,
coach houses and stables
surrounded by beautiful
gardens and patios.

### Hotel Barrosa Palace, Chiclana de la Frontera

MAP B5 ▪ Novo Sancti
Petri ▪ 956 49 22 00
▪ www.hipotels.com/
hotel-barrosa-palace-en-
cadiz.htm ▪ Disabled
access ▪ €€€
A spa-resort right on the
beach, just south of Cádiz.
It has three restaurants, a
fitness centre, indoor and
outdoor pools and a range
of beauty treatments.

### Hotel Jerez, Jerez

MAP B5 ▪ Avda Álvaro
Domecq 35 ▪ 956 30 06 00
▪ www.hace.es ▪ Disabled
access ▪ €€€
Rooms here have been
decorated in a warm style
and overlook the gardens.
All have satellite TV and
Internet; many also have a
Jacuzzi. There's a spa and
wellness centre too.

### Vincci Selección Aleysa, Benalmádena

MAP D5 ▪ Avda Antonio
Machado 57 ▪ 952 56 65
66 ▪ www.vinccihoteles.
com ▪ Disabled access
▪ €€€
This boutique hotel on the
beachfront has great sea
views. There's a wellness
spa and healthy activities
including free yoga and
pilates in the garden.

## Resorts

### Barceló Jerez, Montecastillo

MAP B5 ▪ Ctra Jerez-
Arcos km 6 ▪ 956 15 12
04 ▪ www.hotelbarcelo
montecastillo.com
▪ Disabled access ▪ €€
Towering like a castle of
pale yellow stucco beside
one of Europe's top golf
courses, the hotel gives
lots of activity, eating and
drinking options.

### Hotel Playa de la Luz, Rota

MAP B5 ▪ Avda de la
Diputación ▪ 956 81 05
00 ▪ www.hace.es/en/
hotelplayadelaluz
▪ Disabled access ▪ €€
Most rooms have a terrace
or balcony at this hotel,
nestled by an unspoiled
beach. Minimum two- or
three-night stay during
peak seasons.

### Barceló la Bobadilla, Granada

MAP E4 ▪ Carretera
Salinas-Villanueva de
Tapia (A333) km 65.5
▪ 958 32 18 61 ▪ www.
barcelolabobadilla.com
▪ €€€
Fabulous and reminiscent
of a tiny Moorish village
with its own chapel,
gardens and patios.

### Hotel La Fuente de la Higuera, Ronda

MAP D5 ▪ Partido de los
Frontones ▪ 952 16 56 08
▪ www.hotellafuente.com
▪ Disabled access ▪ €€€
Set in a renovated olive
oil mill where Spanish
architecture meets Post-
Modern design. Rooms
have individually designed
interiors and a garden
area or terrace. There's
also an outdoor pool.

### Hotel Fuerte Conil, Conil de la Frontera

MAP B5 ▪ Playa de la
Fontanilla ▪ 956 44 33 44
▪ www.fuertehoteles.com
▪ Closed Nov–Feb
▪ Disabled access ▪ €€€
An award-winner for
its environmentally
friendly practices, this
Neo-Moorish-style
resort is not far from the
fishing village of Conil.
There's a choice of rest-
aurants, a pool, spa and
sports facilities.

*For a key to hotel price categories see p140*

### Hotel Paraíso del Mar, Nerja
MAP E5 ▪ C/Prolongación de Carabeo 22 ▪ 952 52 16 21 ▪ www.hotel paraisodelmar.es
▪ Disabled access ▪ €€€
All rooms have a Jacuzzi and enjoy views of either the beach, the mountains or the hotel's gardens.

### Hotel Vincci Rumaykiyya, Sierra Nevada, Monachil
MAP F4 ▪ Urb. Sol y Nieve s/n ▪ 958 48 25 08 ▪ www. vinccihoteles.com ▪ Closed mid-Apr–Dec ▪ €€€
With an alpine-style decor, this hotel is at the heart of the ski resort. There's a chair lift service at its door.

### Isla Cristina Palace & Spa, Isla Cristina
MAP A4 ▪ Avda del Parque s/n ▪ 959 34 44 99 ▪ www.sensimarisla cristinapalace.com
▪ Disabled access ▪ €€€
Enjoy beachfront access and a range of massages, Turkish baths and saunas. All rooms have balconies.

### Kempinski Resort Hotel, Estepona
MAP D5 ▪ Ctra de Cádiz km 159 ▪ 952 80 95 00 ▪ www.kempinski-spain. com ▪ Disabled access ▪ €€€
A magnificent resort with a whimsical take on Moorish and regional architecture that suits the seaside setting perfectly.

### Marriott Marbella Beach Resort
MAP D5 ▪ Marbella del Este, Ctra. de Cádiz km 193 ▪ 952 76 96 00 ▪ www.marriott.com
▪ Disabled access ▪ €€€
Surrounded by lush gardens with multiple pools, a great gym, sauna and plenty of activities to keep children amused.

## Historic Finds

### Amanhavis Hotel, Benahavis, Málaga
MAP D5 ▪ C/Pilar 3 ▪ 952 85 60 26/61 51 ▪ www. amanhavis.com ▪ Closed mid-Jan–mid-Feb ▪ €€
This place is like an Andalucian theme park, albeit very tasteful. Rooms are linked to an episode in Spanish history, such as Boabdil or Christopher Columbus, and styled accordingly. Free Wi-Fi.

### La Casa Grande, Arcos de la Frontera
MAP C5 ▪ C/Maldonado 10 ▪ 956 70 39 30 ▪ www.lacasagrande.net ▪ Closed 6 Jan–6 Feb ▪ €€
In 1729, the Nuñez de Prado family erected this mansion. Perched on the cliff of La Peña, it features ceramic tiles, stone columns, wood beams and antiques. Free Wi-Fi.

### Hacienda de Orán, Utrera
MAP C4 ▪ Ctra A8029 km 7 ▪ 955 81 59 94 ▪ www. haciendadeoran.com
▪ Disabled access ▪ €€
This stately 17th-century Andalucian manor is decorated with antiques and rich textiles. There are bougainvillea-covered porches, horse stables, a carriage museum, a pool and even a small airstrip.

### Hotel Convento Aracena
MAP B3 ▪ C/Jesus y Maria 19 ▪ 959 12 68 99 ▪ €€
Housed in a 17th-century convent, this hotel has an outdoor pool as well as a spa and wellness centre. Buffet breakfast. Bike hire available at the reception.

### Hotel Puerta de la Luna, Baeza
MAP F2 ▪ Canónigo Melgares Raya s/n ▪ 953 74 70 19 ▪ www. hotelpuertadelaluna.com
▪ Disabled access ▪ €€
A 16th-century building in the heart of old Baeza. Rooms are each uniquely furnished. Free Wi-Fi and an outdoor pool.

### Palacio de la Rambla, Úbeda
MAP F2 ▪ Plaza del Marqués 1 ▪ 953 75 01 96 ▪ www.palaciode larambla.com ▪ €€
This 16th-century palace offers eight rooms for guests to experience the refined atmosphere. The patio is said to have been designed by the architect Andrés de Vandelvira.

### Sercotel Hotel Monasterio San Miguel, El Puerto de Santa María
MAP B5 ▪ C/Virgen de los Milagros 27 ▪ 956 54 04 40 ▪ en.sanmiguel hotelmonasterio.com
▪ Disabled access ▪ €€
This former monastery, with Baroque architecture and art, is equipped with modern luxuries including an excellent restaurant, a pool and a solarium.

### Hotel Hacienda Posada de Vallina, Córdoba
MAP D3 ▪ C/Corregidor Luis de la Cerda 83 ▪ 957 49 87 50 ▪ www.hhposa dadevallina.es ▪ Disabled access ▪ €€€
In the heart of Córdoba's Jewish Quarter, this charming, historic hotel

retains original features, including beamed ceilings and exposed stone walls.

## NH Amistad Córdoba

MAP D3 ▪ Plaza de Maimónides 3 ▪ 957 42 03 35 ▪ www.nh-hotels. com ▪ Disabled access ▪ €€€

Minutes from La Mezquita and built into the old city walls. The large patio-cloisters are lovely, and there's also a plunge pool and sun terrace. Free Wi-Fi.

## El Poeta de Ronda

MAP D5 ▪ C/Tenorio 1, Ronda ▪ 952 87 01 01 ▪ www.hotelpoeta.es ▪ Disabled access ▪ €€€

This elegant mansion was once the home of the poet Pedro Pérez Clotet. The 12 rooms are tastefully decorated with handmade furniture. Free Wi-Fi.

## Budget Charmers

## Casa Puerta del Sol Corredera, Arcos de la Frontera

MAP C5 ▪ C/Corredera 43 ▪ 956 70 03 94 ▪ www. casaruralpuertadelsol. com ▪ €

This intimate and stylish hotel, with five en-suite rooms, is located close to several historic sites. There's also a good café on-site. Free Wi-Fi.

## Hosteria Lineros 38, Córdoba

MAP D3 ▪ C/Lineros 38 ▪ 957 48 25 17 ▪ www. hosterialineros38.com ▪ Disabled access ▪ €

With its striking Mudéjar-style architecture, this building epitomizes the city's cross-cultural charm. It's a great choice in the old quarter. Free Wi-Fi.

## Hotel Doña Blanca, Jerez de la Frontera

MAP B5 ▪ C/Bodegas 11 ▪ 956 34 87 61 ▪ www. hoteldonablanca.com ▪ €

For the price, this place provides all the services you'd expect of more high-end properties. The rooms are basic, but perfectly maintained, and there's parking and free Wi-Fi.

## Hotel Embarcadero de Calahonda de Granada

MAP F5 ▪ C/Biznaga 14 ▪ 958 62 30 11 ▪ www. embarcaderodecala honda.com ▪ Disabled access ▪ €

Set right on the beach in the picturesque village of Calahonda, this hotel has stylish, well-equipped rooms. Excellent restaurant on-site. Free Wi-Fi.

## Hotel González, Córdoba

MAP D3 ▪ C/Manriquez 3 ▪ 957 47 98 19 ▪ www. hotel-gonzalez.com ▪ €

This charming hotel typifies the old houses of the Jewish Quarter, with a central patio and an elegant marble entrance replete with antiques and high ceilings. The narrow streets of the Quarter make access by car a little difficult. Free Wi-Fi.

## Hotel San Gabriel, Ronda

MAP D5 ▪ C/Marqués de Moctezuma 19 ▪ 952 19 03 92 ▪ www. hotelsangabriel.com ▪ Closed 1–9 Jan, 19–31 Jul & 21–31 Dec ▪ €

Built in 1736, this converted mansion, with its original coat of arms and handsome façade, offers sumptuous rooms for the price.

## Pension Miguel, Nerja

MAP E5 ▪ C/Almirante Ferrandiz 31 ▪ 952 52 15 23 ▪ www.pension miguel.net ▪ €

A family-run hostel in the heart of Nerja, convenient for restaurants and bars in the village. It is taste-fully decorated with a Moroccan theme. Rooms are comfortable and have ceiling fans, fridges and are en-suite. There is a delightful roof terrace.

## Hotel Argantonio, Cádiz

MAP B5 ▪ C/Argantonio 3, Cádiz ▪ 956 21 16 40 ▪ www.hotelargantonio. es ▪ Disabled access ▪ €€

Located in the old town, each floor of this hotel is decorated with a different theme. All rooms have a bath, a flat-screen TV and free Wi-Fi. Some rooms have balconies.

## Hotel La Casa del Califa, Vejer de la Frontera

MAP C6 ▪ Plaza de España 16 ▪ 956 44 77 30 ▪ www.lacasadelcalifa. com ▪ €€

A sojourn at this hotel, created out of eight different houses including the 17th-century Casa del Juzgado, is like staying in a private house. Excellent views and service and a recommended restaurant.

## Hotel TRH, Baeza

MAP F2 ▪ C/Concepción 3 ▪ 953 74 81 30 ▪ www. trhhoteles.com ▪ Disabled access ▪ €€

Right in the heart of this Renaissance town is this oasis of quiet beauty. It's part of a chain, with all the conveniences, yet evokes timeless style.

*For a key to hotel price categories see p140*

## Rural Retreats

### Alcázar de la Reina, Carmona

MAP C3 ▪ Hermana Concepción Orellana 2 ▪ 954 19 62 00 ▪ www.alcazar-reina.es ▪ €

In the historic centre of this small town, the façade of this hotel stands out, while the interior reflects Mudéjar craftsmanship. No two rooms are alike, but they all have marble bathrooms and several offer spectacular views.

### Alquería de los Lentos, Niguelas

MAP F4 ▪ Camino de los Molinos ▪ 958 77 78 50 ▪ www.alqueria deloslentos.com ▪ €

Surrounded by orchards at the foothills of the Sierra Nevada, this 16th-century mill has been lovingly transformed into a small hotel and organic restaurant. There is a swimming pool, and most rooms have terraces.

### Casa Don Carlos, Málaga

MAP D5 ▪ Ctra Coin Churriana km 3.5, Alhaurin el Grande ▪ 669 94 50 46 ▪ www.casadoncarlos.com ▪ €

This award-winning bed and breakfast, facing Alhaurin el Grande, has magnificent views of the countryside. The rooms are clean and comfortable. Guests can hire cars and motorcycles.

### Cuevas La Granja, near Benalúa

MAP F3 ▪ Camino de la Granja ▪ 958 67 60 00 ▪ www.cuevas.org ▪ €

A complex of restored cave dwellings, each of which preserves their original style. It is the perfect setting for rest and relaxation.

### Hacienda La Vereda, Montilla

MAP D3 ▪ Vereda del Cerro Macho ▪ 957 33 53 01 ▪ www.haciendalavereda.es ▪ Disabled access ▪ €

Encompassed by gardens and vineyards, this tranquil country manor is an ideal place to unwind by the pool, go horse riding or tour the vineyards.

### Villa Los Paraisos, La Puebla de Cazalla

MAP C4 ▪ Los Abrigosos ▪ 956 68 49 03 ▪ www.villalosparaisos.co.uk ▪ €

This charming, award-winning bed and breakfast is just a short drive from Seville. The villa is set in a wonderful location and provides a perfect setting for bird-watching and cycling. The owner is quite gracious and an excellent cook.

### La Almendra y el Gitano, Almería

MAP G4 ▪ Camino Cala del Plomo, Agua Amarga ▪ 678 50 29 11 ▪ www.laalmendray elgitano.com ▪ €€

In the heart of a natural park, close to unspoilt beaches, and with no phones or Internet, this is a haven of tranquillity.

### Antonio, Zahara de los Atunes

MAP C6 ▪ Atlanterra km 1 ▪ 956 43 91 41 ▪ www.antoniohoteles.com ▪ Disabled access ▪ €€

This seaside retreat is decorated in a traditional style, with whitewashed walls, and there's a nice pool. Most rooms have terraces with sea views.

### Cortijo El Sotillo, San José

MAP H5 ▪ Ctra Entrada a San José ▪ 950 61 11 00 ▪ www.cortijoelsotillo.com ▪ Disabled access ▪ €€

A tranquil base from which to explore the beaches of Cabo de Gata. The rooms here are spacious and have large terraces with beautiful views.

### Finca Buen Vino, Sierra de Aracena

MAP B3 ▪ Los Marines, N433 km95 ▪ 959 12 40 34 ▪ www.fincabuenvino.com ▪ €€

A converted ranch, set amid green hills, this bed and breakfast is filled with an eclectic mix of furniture, paintings, pottery and books. Rooms are all distinctive, with Oriental hangings, a bathtub with a view, or a fireplace. Self-catering cottages also available.

## Hostels, Camping and Self-Catered

### Albergue Inturjoven, Marbella

MAP D5 ▪ C/Trapiche 2 ▪ 955 03 58 86 ▪ www.inturjoven.com ▪ Disabled access ▪ €

Double rooms, some with adjoining bath, a pool and recreational options make this an excellent youth hostel. It's just north of the lovely Casco Antiguo (old quarter), where you can see the real Marbella. Walk through its narrow, cobbled streets to get to the beach and the port.

### Camping Cabo de Gata, Cabo de Gata

MAP H5 ▪ Ctra Cabo de Gata, Cortijo Ferrón ▪ 950 16 04 43 ▪ www. campingcabodegata.com ▪ Disabled access ▪ €

This campsite offers shady areas for tents, trailers and RV hook-ups, as well as bungalows. Facilities include a pool, access to pristine beaches and a reception centre with safes. Credit cards are not accepted.

### Camping Sierra Nevada, Granada

MAP F4 ▪ Avda de Madrid 107 ▪ 958 15 00 62 ▪ www.campingsierra nevada.com ▪ Closed Nov–Feb ▪ Disabled access ▪ €

One of the most convenient camping choices in the region, with big, clean bathrooms, a pool and a laundry. There is also a budget motel on the site. (No credit cards.)

### Camping El Sur, Ronda

MAP D5 ▪ Ctra Ronda-Algeciras km 1.5 ▪ 952 87 59 39 ▪ www.camping elsur.com ▪ Disabled access ▪ €

Camping and bungalows with kitchen and bathroom are available here. It's a chance to take beautiful walks or horse ride in the countryside around Ronda.

### Casas Rurales Benarum, Mecina Bombarón

MAP F4 ▪ C/ Casas Blancas 1 ▪ 958 851 149 ▪ www.benarum.com ▪ €

Twelve rural cabins, each housing two to five people, nestle in this quiet mountain town. The cabins are fully equipped and there is a pool and spa on-site.

### Los Castillarejos Apartamentos Rurales, Córdoba

MAP D3 ▪ Ctra CO-6203 km 5.7, Luque ▪ 957 09 00 12 ▪ www. loscastillarejos.com ▪ Disabled access ▪ €

A set of 14 modern apartments decorated using natural materials and local stone. Kitchens are fully equipped; there's a pool and free Wi-Fi.

### Hostal la Fuente, Córdoba

MAP D3 ▪ C/San Fernando 51 ▪ 957 48 78 27 ▪ www.hostallafuente. com ▪ €

A charming budget hotel in the centre of Córdoba, offering single, double, triple and quadruple rooms as well as some apartments. There's a roof-top terrace with an adjoining café, a central courtyard and a large communal lounge.

### Hostal La Malagueña, Estepona

MAP D5 ▪ C/Castillo 1 ▪ 952 80 00 11 ▪ www. hlmestepona.com ▪ €

Although it isn't an official hostel or even aimed at backpackers, the price doesn't get any better than this. The airy rooms have balconies facing the square. You can stroll along the sandy beaches or wander around the shops of this old and still authentic fishing village.

### Hostal La Posada, Mijas

MAP D5 ▪ C/Coin 47 & 49 ▪ 952 48 53 10 ▪ €

Rent a fully equipped apartment in this white village and sample a bit of the real Andalucía. Not all have air conditioning.

### Instalación Juvenil, Sol y Nieve, Sierra Nevada

MAP F4 ▪ C/Peñones 22 ▪ 955 03 58 86 ▪ www.inturjoven.com ▪ Disabled access ▪ €

Located near the top of the ski station, with rooms holding two to six, this place is ideal for skiers in the winter or trekkers in the summer. Skis and other equipment for hire.

### Torre de la Peña, Tarifa

MAP C6 ▪ Ctra N340, Tarifa ▪ 956 68 49 03 ▪ www.campingtp.com ▪ €€

This hotel offers beach-front camping and bungalows, with spectacular views. It is perfect for windsurfing, kitesurfing and snorkelling. There's a good restaurant on-site.

### Cantueso, Periana

MAP E4 ▪ Periana, Málaga ▪ 699 94 62 13 ▪ www.cantueso.net ▪ Limited disabled access ▪ €€

Ten whitewashed cottages with private terraces enjoy a splendid mountainside setting. Lush gardens provide tranquillity. Not all have air conditioning.

### Casas Karen, Costa de la Luz

MAP C6 ▪ 9 Fuente del Madroño 6, nr Cabo Trafalgar ▪ 956 43 70 67 ▪ www.casaskaren.com ▪ €€

Typical Andalucian *chozas* (traditional, thatched straw bungalows) and converted farm buildings between pine woods and the beach. Follow signs to Faro de Trafalgar.

# Index

# Acknowledgments

## Author

American-born Jeffrey Kennedy now lives mainly in Italy and Spain. A graduate of Stanford University, he divides his time between producing, acting and writing. He is the co-author of *Top 10 Rome* and the author of the Top 10 guides to *Mallorca, Miami and the Keys* and *San Francisco*.

**Additional contributor**
Chris Moss

**Publishing Director** Georgina Dee
**Publisher** Vivien Antwi
**Design Director** Phil Ormerod
**Editorial** Michelle Crane, Rachel Fox, Freddie Marriage, Jayne Miller, Sally Schafer
**Design** Richard Czapnik, Marisa Renzullo
**Commissioned Photography** Neil Lukas, Rough Guides/Demetrio Carrasco, Clive Streeter, Peter Wilson
**Picture Research** Susie Peachey, Ellen Root, Lucy Sienkowska, Oran Tarjan
**Cartography** Zafar-ul Islam Khan, Suresh Kumar, James Macdonald, Casper Morris
**DTP** Jason Little, George Nimmo
**Production** Nancy-Jane Maun
**Factchecker** Lynnette McCurdy Bastida
**Proofreader** Kathryn Glendenning
**Indexer** Helen Peters
**Illustrator** chrisorr.com

First edition created by Sargasso Media Ltd, London

**Revisions team**
Parnika Bagla, Lucy Richards, Vinita Venugopal

## Picture Credits

The publisher would like to thank the following for their kind permission to reproduce their photographs:
**Key:** a-above; b-below/bottom; c-centre; f-far; l-left; r-right; t-top

**Alamy Stock Photo:** a-plus image bank 15bl; age fotostock/Alberto Paredes 128tl, /Alvaro Leiva 71crb, /Francisco Barba 26br, /Rafael Campillo 73cl, /J.D. Dallet 122cl, /Juan José Pascual 57cr, 125tr; Guillermo Aguilar 14bl; Jerónimo Alba 54cr, 62-3, 79clb, 80b; Peter Barritt 48cl; Artur Bogacki 65cl; Tibor Bognar 11cr, 34bl; Bon Appetit/FoodPhotogr. Eising 77tr; Charles Bowman 64tl; Michelle Chaplow 72br, 121tr; classicpaintings 48tr; Stuart Crump HDR 69tr; Felipe Caparros Cruz 50b; Design Pics Inc/Ken Welsh 44tc; Ilja Dubovskis 99cb; Robert Fried 91c; geogphotos 66tl; Kevin George 90cl; Hemis.fr/Bruno Morandi 46t, /Bertrand Reiger 22crb; Heritage Image Partnership Ltd/Werner Forman Archive 45c; Peter Horree 108cla; imageBROKER/Egon Bömsch 35cl, /White Star/Monica Gumm 73br; imageimage 81tr; Jam World Images 52cla, 56cl, 61tr, 98b; John Kellerman 18bl, 87cl; LOOK Die Bildagentur der Fotografen GmbH/Ingolf Pompe 110bl; Jose Lucas 47cl; Cro Magnon 99tr; Clement McCarthy 46bl; Angus McComiskey 7t; Tim Moore 128bc; Hilary Morgan 55crb; Perry van Munster 113clb; myLAM 129cr; Peter Netley 39clb; Sean Pavone 22-3, 108br; philipus 95tl; Ingolf Pompe 87 112tl; QEDimages 48bc; Rolf Richardson 49clb; Robert Harding Productions 47tr; Rolf Hicker Photography 58br, 116tr; Saaaaa 95crb; Pascal Saez 38-9, 80cla; Scott Rylander Stage 49br; Carmen Sedano 110crca; Gordon Sinclair 77cl; Michael Sparrow 60br; Ivan Vdovin 97cl; Bax Walker 111cr; Ken Welsh 21cr, 70cl; Tony West 39cr; Wiskerke 54bl; World History Archive 43tl.

**Bridgeman Images:** 43br.

**Consejería de Turismo, Comercio y Deportes de la Junta de Andalucia:** 4t, 13cr, 17t, 24cl, 24cr.

**Corbis:** Nano Calvo 45tl; EPA/ Julio Munez 91tl; the food passionates/ Hendrik Holler 76t; Owen Franken 76clb; Hemis/Patrick Escudero 4cla; JAI/Alan Copson 28-9; Katja Kreder 42cr; Ocean/Marco Brivio 53crb.

**Dreamstime.com:** Adreslebedev 78tr; Alexsalcedo 79tr; David Acosta Allely 26clb; Amoklv 1, 32clb; Angellodeco 72cla; Arenaphotouk 34cr, 35tc, 35crb, 38bl, 51cla, 51crb, 100bc, 106clb; Artur Bogacki 24bc, 25tc, 106tl; Boris Breytman 31tl; Paul Brighton 74cl; Gunold Brunbauer 4clb; Ryhor Bruyeu 69cl, Carpaumar 94tl, Dulsita 3tr, 130-1, Shchipkova Elena 10crb, Serban Enache 104b; Iakov Filimonov 7cra, 96br; Fotomicar 61cl; Jordi Clave Garsot 18cr; Grantotufo 96tl; Silvia Blaszczyszyn Jakiello 86cl; Lukasz Janyst 33tc; Jesole 27tl; Kiko Jiménez 57tl, 86br; Joserpizarro 2tr, 40-1, 68t; Marcin Jucha 75tr; Karelgallas 60t; Vichaya Kiatying-angsulee 4crb, 21t, 86tl; Karol Kozlowski 12bl, 16cr, 59t, 104tl; Dmitry Kushch 44b; Emanuele Leoni 10cl, 14tl, 19tl; Elisa Locci 26-7, Lotsostock 16tl; Lunamarina 4b, 65br; Dariya Maksimova 98cra; Mardym 78b; Brian Maudsley 25cr; minnystock 30-1, 117c;

Elena Moiseeva 74br; Moskwa 105cl;; Juan Moyano 32-3, 58cl, 74tr, 119clb; Aitor Muñoz Muñoz 127cl; Carlos Neto 31bl; Pathastings 75cla; Sean Pavone 2tl, 3tl, 4cl, 8-9, 30cl, 82-3, 85tl, 114-5; Perseomedusa 6cra; Pigprox 89cra; Yuan Ping 11tl; Ppy2010ha 75clb; Rangpl 32br; Alvaro Trabazo Rivas 107cl; Fesus Robert 103tl; Paloma Rodriguez De Los Rios Ramirez 118t; Rubenconpi 12cla; Sborisov 12-3, 19br; Jozef Sedmak 49tl, 52b, 84tl, 88tl, 118cl; Sergeialyoshin 10-1; Iryna Soltyska 23bl, 33cr; Jose I. Soto 13clb, 15cr, 16br; Alena Stalmashonak 20r; Nick Stubbs 11br, 39tl, 64b; Jan Sučko 11cra; Titelio 10cla; Aleksandar Todorovic 20cl, 42b, 50tr, 85br; Typhoonski 27bl; Venemama 68br; Alvaro German Vilela 10clb; Yury 124cl; Vladimir Zhuravlev 71t; Zoom-zoom 45br.

**El Rinconcillo:** 92t.

**Getty Images:** Imagno 43clb; Holger Leue 101c; Moment 67cl; NIS/Diego Lopez Alvarez 36-7; David Ramos 81cl; UIG/Editorial Education Images 36b.

**Ministerio de Agricultura, Alimentación y Medio Ambiente Gabinete de la Ministra:** 11clb, 36cl; CENEAM - MMA/J.M. Reyero 36crb, 37tc, 37crb.

**Museo Torre de la Calahorra:** 23cb.

**Museo Parque de las Ciencias:** 55t.

**Real Alcázar de Sevilla:** 21clb.

**Rex by Shutterstock:** imageBROKER/Stefan Kiefer 67tr.

**Robert Harding Picture Library:** age fotostock/Daniel Sanz 6br; J.D. Dallet 22cl; Anna Elias 126tr; Jose Fuste Raga 126b; Sylvain Grandadam 93clb; Guy Heitmann 102tl; Jose Lucas 120cr; Guy Thouvenin 89bl; Ben Welsh 66bl; Michael Zegers 100tl.

**Sollo:** Food & Groove 113ca.

**SuperStock:** Iberfoto 124tr.

**Real Club Valderrama:** 109tr.

**Cover**

Front and spine: **AWL Images:** Alan Copson.

Back: **Dreamstime.com:** Lunamarina.

**Pull Out Map Cover**

**AWL Images:** Alan Copson.

All other images © Dorling Kindersley

For further information see:
www.dkimages.com

Penguin Random House

Printed and bound in China

First American Edition, 2004
Published in the United States by
DK Publishing, 345 Hudson Street,
New York, New York 10014

Copyright 2004, 2017 © Dorling
Kindersley Limited

A Penguin Random House Company

16 17 18 19 10 9 8 7 6 5 4 3 2 1

**Reprinted with revisions 2006, 2008, 2010, 2012, 2014, 2016**

Published in Great Britain by Dorling Kindersley Limited.

A catalog record for this book is available from the Library of Congress.

ISSN 1479-344X.
ISBN 978 1 4654 5736 3

MIX
Paper from responsible sources
FSC™ C018179

**SPECIAL EDITIONS OF DK TRAVEL GUIDES**

DK Travel Guides can be purchased in bulk quantities at discounted prices for use in promotions or as premiums. We are also able to offer special editions and personalized jackets, corporate imprints, and excerpts from all of our books, tailored specifically to meet your own needs.

To find out more, please contact:

in the US
specialsales@dk.com

in the UK
travelguides@uk.dk.com

in Canada
specialmarkets@dk.com

in Australia
penguincorporatesales@
penguinrandomhouse.com.au

*As a guide to abbreviations in visitor information blocks: **Adm** = admission charge; **DA** = disabled access; **D** = dinner; **L** = lunch.*

# Phrase Book

## In an Emergency

| | | |
|---|---|---|
| Help! | ¡Socorro! | soh-koh-roh |
| Stop! | ¡Pare! | pah-reh |
| Call... | ¡Llame a... | yah-meh ah |
| ...a doctor! | ...un médico! | oon meh-dee-koh |
| ...an ambulance! | ...una ambulancia! | oonah ahm-boo-lahn-thee-ah |
| ...the police! | ...la policia! | lah poh-lee-thee-ah |
| ...the fire brigade! | ...los bomberos! | lohs bohm-beh-rohs |
| | | |
| Where is... | ¿Dónde está... | dohn-deh ehs-tah |
| ...the nearest telephone? | ...el teléfono más próximo? | ehl teh-leh-foh-noh mahs prohx-ee-moh |
| ...the nearest hospital? | ...el hospital más próximo? | ehl ohs pee-tahl mahs prohx-ee-moh |

## Communication Essentials

| | | |
|---|---|---|
| Yes | Sí | see |
| No | No | noh |
| Please | Por favor | pohr fah-vohr |
| Thank you | Gracias | grah-thee-ahs |
| Excuse me | Perdone | pehr-doh-neh |
| Hello | Hola | oh-lah |
| Goodbye | Adiós | ah-dee-ohs |
| Good night | Buenas noches | bweh-nahs noh-chehs |
| | | |
| Morning | La mañana | lah mah-nyah-nah |
| Afternoon/Evening | La tarde | lah tahr-deh |
| Yesterday | Ayer | ah-yehr |
| Today | Hoy | oy |
| Tomorrow | Mañana | mah-nya-nah |
| Here | Aquí | ah-kee |
| There | Allí | ah-yee |
| What? | ¿Qué? | keh |
| When? | ¿Cuándo? | kwahn-doh |
| Why? | ¿Por qué? | pohr-keh |
| Where? | ¿Dónde? | dohn-deh |

## Useful Phrases

| | | |
|---|---|---|
| How are you? | ¿Cómo está usted? | koh-moh ehs-tah oos-tehd |
| Very well, thank you | Muy bien, gracias | mwee bee-ehn grah-thee-ahs |
| Pleased to meet you. | Encantado de conocerle. | ehn-kahn-tah-doh deh thehr-leh |
| See you soon | Hasta pronto | ahs-tah-prohn-toh |
| That's fine | Está bien | ehs-tah bee-ehn |
| Where is/are...? | ¿Dónde está/están...? | dohn-deh ehs-tah/ehs-tahn |
| How far is it to...? | Cuántos metros/kilómetros hay de aquí a...? | kwahn-tohs meh-trohs/kee-loh-meh-trohs eye deh ah-kee ah |
| Which way to...? | ¿Por dónde se va a...? | pohr dohn-deh seh bah ah |
| Do you speak English? | ¿Habla inglés? | ah-blah een-glehs |
| I don't understand | No comprendo | noh kohm-prehn-doh |
| Could you speak more slowly please? | ¿Puede hablar más despacio por favor? | pweh-deh ah-blahr mahs dehs-pah-thee-oh pohr fah-vohr |
| I'm sorry | Lo siento | loh see-ehn-toh |

## Useful Words

| | | |
|---|---|---|
| big | grande | grahn-deh |
| small | pequeño | peh-keh-nyoh |
| hot | caliente | kah-lee-ehn-teh |
| cold | frío | free-oh |
| good | bueno | bweh-noh |
| bad | malo | mah-loh |
| well | bien | bee-ehn |
| open | abierto | ah-bee-ehr-toh |
| closed | cerrado | thehr-rah-doh |
| left | izquierda | eeth-key-ehr-dah |
| right | derecha | deh-reh-chah |
| straight on | todo recto | toh-doh rehk-toh |

| | | |
|---|---|---|
| near | cerca | thehr-kah |
| far | lejos | leh-hohs |
| up | arriba | ah-ree-bah |
| down | abajo | ah-bah-hoh |
| early | temprano | tehm-prah-noh |
| late | tarde | tahr-deh |
| entrance | entrada | ehn-trah-dah |
| exit | salida | sah-lee-dah |
| toilet | servicios | sehr-bee-thee-ohs |
| more | más | mahs |
| less | menos | meh-nohs |

## Shopping

| | | |
|---|---|---|
| How much does this cost? | ¿Cuánto cuesta esto? | kwahn-toh kwehs-ta ehs-toh |
| I would like... | Me gustaría... | meh goos-ta-ree-ah |
| Do you have...? | ¿Tienen...? | tee-yeh-nehn |
| Do you take cards? | ¿Aceptan tarjetas? | ah-thehp-tahn tahr-heh-tahs |
| What time do you open/close? | ¿A qué hora abren/cierran? | ah keh oh-rah ah-brehn/thee-ehr-rahn |
| This one | Éste | ehs-teh |
| That one | Ése | eh-seh |
| expensive | caro | kahr-oh |
| cheap | barato | bah-rah-toh |
| size, clothes | talla | tah-yah |
| size, shoes | número | noo-mehr-oh |
| antiques shop | la tienda de antigüedades | tee-ehn-dah deh ahn-tee-gweh-dah-dehs |
| bakery | la panadería | pah-nah-deh-ree-ah |
| bank | el banco | bahn-koh |
| bookshop | la librería | lee-breh-ree-ah |
| cake shop | la pastelería | pahs-teh-leh-ree-ah |
| chemist's | la farmacia | ahr-mah-thee-ah |
| grocer's | la tienda de comestibles | tee-ehn-dah deh koh-mehs-tee-blehs |
| market | el mercado | mehr-kah-doh |
| newsagent's | el kiosko de prensa | kee-ohs-koh deh prehn-sah |
| post office | la oficina de correos | oh-fee-thee-nah deh korh-reh-ohs |
| shoe shop | la zapatería | thah-pah-teh-ree-ah |
| supermarket | el super-mercado | soo-pehr-mehr-kah-doh |
| travel agency | la agencia de viajes | ah-hehn-thee-ah -deh beeah-hehs |

## Sightseeing

| | | |
|---|---|---|
| art gallery | el museo de arte | moo-seh-oh deh ahr-teh |
| cathedral | la catedral | kah-teh-drahl |
| church | la iglesia, la basílica | ee-gleh-see-ah bah-see lee-kah |
| garden | el jardín | hahr-deen |
| library | la biblioteca | bee-blee-oh-teh-kah |
| museum | el museo | moo-seh-oh |
| tourist information office | la oficina de turismo | oh-fee-thee nah deh too-rees-moh |
| town hall | el ayunta-miento | ah-yoon-toh mee-ehn-toh |
| bus station | la estación de autobuses | ehs-tah-thee-ohn deh owtoh-boo-sehs |
| railway station | la estación de trenes | ehs-tah-thee-ohn deh treh-nehs |

## Staying in a Hotel

| | | |
|---|---|---|
| Do you have a vacant room? | ¿Tiene una habitación libre? | tee-eh-neh oo-nah ah-bee- tah-thee-ohn lee-breh |
| double room | habitación doble | ah-bee-tah-thee-ohn doh-bleh |
| with double bed | con cama de matrimonio | kohn kah-mah deh mah-tree-moh-nee-oh |
| twin room | habitación con dos camas | ah-bee-tah-thee-ohn kohn dohs kah-mahs |

| single room | habitación individual | ah-bee-tah-thee-ohn een-dee-vee-doo-ahl |
| room with a bath | habitación con baño | ah-bee-tah-thee-ohn kohn bah-nyoh |
| porter | el botones | boh-toh-nehs |
| key | la llave | yah-veh |
| I have a reservation | Tengo una habitación reservada | tehn-goh oo-na ah-bee-tah-thee-ohn reh-sehr-bah-dah |

## Eating Out

| Have you got a table for…? | ¿Tiene mesa para…? | tee-eh-neh meh-sah pah pah-rah |
| I want to reserve a table | Quiero reservar una mesa | kee-eh-roh reh-sehr-bahr oo-nah meh-sah |
| the bill | La cuenta | kwehn-tah |
| I am a vegetarian | Soy vegetariano/a | soy beh-heh-tah-ree-ah-no/na |
| waitress/ waiter | camarera/ camarero | kah-mah-reh-rah/ kah-mah-reh-roh |
| menu | la carta | kahr-tah |
| fixed-price menu | menú del día | meh-noo dehl dee-ah |
| wine list | la carta de vinos | kahr-tah deh bee-nohs |
| glass | un vaso | bah-soh |
| bottle | una botella | boh-teh-yah |
| knife | un cuchillo | koo-chee-yoh |
| fork | un tenedor | teh-neh-dohr |
| spoon | una cuchara | koo-chah-rah |
| breakfast | el desayuno | deh-sah-yoo-noh |
| lunch | la comida/ el almuerzo | koh-mee-dah/ ahl-mwehr-thoh |
| dinner | la cena | theh-nah |
| main course | el primer plato | pree-mehr plah-toh |
| starters | los entremeses | ehn-treh-meh-ses |
| dish of the day | el plato del día | plah-toh dehl dee-ah |
| coffee | el café | kah-feh |
| rare (meat) | poco hecho | poh-koh eh-choh |
| medium | medio hecho | meh-dee-oh eh-choh |
| well done | muy hecho | mwee eh-choh |

## Menu Decoder

| al horno | ahl ohr-noh | baked |
| asado | ah-sah-doh | roast |
| el aceite | ah-thee-eh-teh | oil |
| las aceitunas | ah-theh-toon-ahs | olives |
| el agua mineral | ah-gwa mee-neh-rahl | mineral water |
| sin gas/con gas | seen gas/kohn gas | still/sparkling |
| el ajo | ah-hoh | garlic |
| el arroz | ah-rohth | rice |
| el azúcar | ah-thoo-kahr | sugar |
| la carne | kahr-neh | meat |
| la cebolla | theh-boh-yah | onion |
| el cerdo | therh-doh | pork |
| la cerveza | thehr-beh-thah | beer |
| el chocolate | choh-koh-lah-teh | chocolate |
| el chorizo | choh-ree-thoh | spicy sausage |
| el cordero | kohr-deh-roh | lamb |
| frito | free-toh | fried |
| la fruta | froo-tah | fruit |
| los frutos secos | froo-tohs seh-kohs | nuts |
| las gambas | gahm-bahs | prawns |
| el helado | eh-lah-doh | ice cream |
| el huevo | oo-eh-voh | egg |
| el jamón serrano | hah-mohn sehr-rah-noh | cured ham |
| la langosta | lahn-gohs-tah | lobster |
| la leche | leh-cheh | milk |
| el limón | lee-mohn | lemon |
| la mantequilla | mahn-teh-kee-yah | butter |
| la manzana | mahn-thah-nah | apple |
| los mariscos | mah-rees-kohs | seafood |
| la naranja | nah-rahn-hah | orange |
| el pan | pahn | bread |

| el pastel | pahs-tehl | pastry |
| las patatas | pah-tah-tahs | potatoes |
| el pescado | pehs-kah-doh | fish |
| la pimienta | pee-mee-yehn-tah | pepper |
| el plátano | plah-tah-noh | banana |
| el pollo | poh-yoh | chicken |
| el postre | pohs-treh | dessert |
| el queso | keh-soh | cheese |
| la sal | sahl | salt |
| la salsa | sahl-sah | sauce |
| seco | seh-koh | dry |
| el solomillo | soh-loh-mee-yoh | sirloin |
| la sopa | soh-pah | soup |
| la tarta | tahr-tah | pie/cake |
| el té | teh | tea |
| la ternera | tehr-neh-rah | beef |
| el vinagre | bee-nah-greh | vinegar |
| el vino blanco | bee-noh blahn-koh | white wine |
| el vino rosado | bee-noh roh-sah-doh | rosé wine |
| el vino tinto | bee-noh teen-toht | red wine |

## Numbers

| 0 | cero | theh-roh |
| 1 | uno | oo-noh |
| 2 | dos | dohs |
| 3 | tres | trehs |
| 4 | cuatro | kwa-troh |
| 5 | cinco | theen-koh |
| 6 | seis | says |
| 7 | siete | see-eh-teh |
| 8 | ocho | oh-choh |
| 9 | nueve | nweh-veh |
| 10 | diez | dee-ehth |
| 11 | once | ohn-theh |
| 12 | doce | doh-theh |
| 13 | trece | treh-theh |
| 14 | catorce | kah-tohr-theh |
| 15 | quince | keen-theh |
| 16 | dieciséis | dee-eh-thee-seh-ees |
| 17 | diecisiete | dee-eh-thee-see-eh-teh |
| 18 | dieciocho | dee-eh-thee-oh-choh |
| 19 | diecinueve | dee-eh-thee-nweh-veh |
| 20 | veinte | beh-een-teh |
| 21 | veintiuno | beh-een-tee-oo-noh |
| 22 | veintidós | beh-een-tee-dohs |
| 30 | treinta | treh-een-tah |
| 31 | treinta y uno | treh-een-tah ee oo-noh |
| 40 | cuarenta | kwah-rehn-tah |
| 50 | cincuenta | theen-kwehn-tah |
| 60 | sesenta | seh-sehn-tah |
| 70 | setenta | seh-tehn-tah |
| 80 | ochenta | oh-chehn-tah |
| 90 | noventa | noh-vehn-tah |
| 100 | cien | thee-ehn |
| 101 | ciento uno | thee-ehn-toh oo-noh |
| 200 | doscientos | dohs-thee-ehn-tohs |
| 500 | quinientos | khee-nee-ehn-tohs |
| 700 | setecientos | seh-teh-thee-ehn-tohs |
| 900 | novecientos | noh-veh-thee-ehn-tohs |
| 1,000 | mil | meel |

## Time

| one minute | un minuto | oon mee-noo-toh |
| one hour | una hora | oo-na oh-rah |
| half an hour | media hora | meh-dee-a oh-rah |
| Monday | lunes | loo-nehs |
| Tuesday | martes | mahr-tehs |
| Wednesday | miércoles | mee-ehr-koh-lehs |
| Thursday | jueves | hoo-weh-vehs |
| Friday | viernes | bee-ehr-nehs |
| Saturday | sábado | sah-bah-doh |
| Sunday | domingo | doh-meen-goh |